Reading the past

Ian Hodder's controversial book focuses on meaning in
archaeology, arguing that the interpretation of
meaning needs to be closely integrated with adaptive,
economic and social factors when we are seeking to
explain the behaviour of past societies. Symbolism and
ideology are discussed in relation to history and social
practice and general accounts are provided of systems
theory in archaeology, of structuralist and Marxist
archaeology, and of the relationships between
archaeology and history. The author then defines what
he has termed contextual and post-processual
archaeology and examines their implications for the
practice of the discipline. In particular, he argues that
while material culture is not a literary text, an analogy
with texts offers powerful insights into the nature of
archaeological data and into the procedures involved in
'reading the past'.

Reading the past

Current approaches to interpretation in archaeology

Ian Hodder

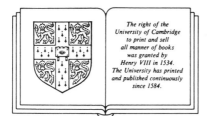

The right of the
University of Cambridge
to print and sell
all manner of books
was granted by
Henry VIII in 1534.
The University has printed
and published continuously
since 1584.

Cambridge University Press

Cambridge

New York   *Port Chester*

Melbourne   *Sydney*

Published by the Press Syndicate of the University of Cambridge
The Pitt Building, Trumpington Street, Cambridge CB2 1RP
40 West 20th Street, New York York, NY 10011, USA
10 Stamford Road, Oakleigh, Melbourne 3166, Australia

First published 1986
Reprinted 1987, 1988, 1989

Printed in Great Britain by Billing and Sons Ltd., Worcester

British Library cataloguing in publication data

Hodder, Ian
Reading the past: current approaches to interpretation in archaeology.
1. Archaeology
I. Title
930.1   CC165

Library of Congress cataloguing in publication data

Hodder, Ian.
Reading the past.
Bibliography.
Includes index.
1. Archaeology–Philosophy.   2. Archaeology–Methodology.   I. Title.
CC72.H62 1986   930.1   86–9637

ISBN 0 521 32743 1 hard covers
ISBN 0 521 33960 X paperback

BO

To Meg

Contents

Preface

In some ways I am surprised that a book of this nature, discussing widely varying theoretical approaches to the past, can be written. In an important article, David Clarke (1973) suggested that archaeology was losing its innocence because it was embracing, in the 1960s and 1970s, a rigorous scientific approach, with agreed sets of procedures, models and theories. The age of unreflecting speculation was over.

However, archaeologists have always claimed to be rigorously scientific. Indeed, I argued (Hodder 1981) that archaeology would remain immature as long as it refused to debate and experiment with a wide range of approaches to the past. In grasping positivism, functionalism, systems theory and so on, and setting itself against alternative perspectives, archaeology remained narrow and out-of-date in comparison with related disciplines.

But over recent years, alternatives have emerged, largely from the European scene (Renfrew 1982), and one can now talk of Marxist and structuralist archaeology, as well as of processual, positivist approaches. Certainly such alternatives existed before, on the fringe, but they did not constitute a distinctive approach with a body of practitioners. The older normative and culture-historical schools also continue to thrive today. While many of these developments, and the erosion of the old 'New Archaeology' debates, have far to go, archaeology is now beginning to lose its innocence and is gaining maturity by being fully integrated into wider contemporary debates. This book seeks to capture this new spirit of debate and to contribute to it from a particular point of view.

At the same time, it seems to me that far from becoming submerged within other disciplines, archaeology has, through the wider debate, become better able to define itself as a distinct and productive area of study. The debate picks out the differences from other disciplines as well as the similarities.

Archaeology is neither 'historical' nor 'anthropological'. It is not even science or art. Archaeology's increasing maturity allows it to claim an independent personality with distinctive qualities to contribute.

Archaeology no longer has to be 'new' and unidirectional, presenting a unified front. It has the maturity to allow diversity, controversy and uncertainty. From catastrophe theory to sociobiology, it is all being applied to the archaeological past. But through this onslaught a more seasoned genre emerges, recapturing the old and redefining the new to form a distinctive archaeological enquiry.

It has become difficult for any one person to grasp the variety of approaches now present in the discipline, and this is my excuse for the inadequacies in my own account. In particular this difficulty contributes to the limited coverage given here of the approaches offered by ecology or palaeoeconomy. Ecological approaches are examined here in relation to systems theory in chapter 2, but for wider-ranging discussion the reader is advised to turn to the excellent accounts provided, for example, by Bailey (1983) and Butzer (1982). I have necessarily adopted a particular standpoint from which to view archaeology. This position is outlined in chapter 1, which concentrates on the nature of cultural meanings and on material culture as meaningfully constituted. Where ecological paradigms have contributed to this debate they have been discussed, but the majority of the work which might fall under that heading is outside the scope of this volume.

That this book is possible is due to the explanatory efforts of numerous researchers, some of whose work I have tried to capture and summarize here. I can only thank them for their inspiration and apologize in advance for any inadequacies of understanding on my part. The criticisms that I have made of their work will, I am sure, be returned in good measure.

While some of the ideas described in this volume were aired to a generation of Cambridge undergraduates, the text initially took form as the content of a graduate seminar course at the State University of New York, Binghamton, in the spring of 1984. The group of students and staff was lively, critical and keen to contribute. The text owes much to the members of the seminar. It was tried out on them and it took shape through their enthusiasm. I thank them, and particularly Meg, for the opportunity and the stimulation.

The final writing was possible while I was a Visiting Lecturer at the University of Paris 1–Sorbonne in 1985. The congenial environment and the critical comments of my friends and colleagues there were invaluable in the preparation of the final manuscript. In particular I wish to thank Serge Cleuziou, Anick Coudart, Jean-Paul Demoule, Mike Illett, Pierre Lemonnier and Alain Schnapp.

1 The problem

Many people are becoming increasingly aware that the so-called New Archaeology of the 60s and early 70s was flawed. However there is little consensus as to the nature and scale of these flaws. It can be claimed that the New Archaeology actually inhibited the development of archaeology itself by trying to subsume it within other realms of study (anthropology and the natural sciences in particular). Despite David Clarke's insistence on 'archaeology is archaeology is archaeology' (1968), his own approach, based on the importation of ideas from statistics, geography and the information sciences, has not led to a viable and distinctive archaeology.

Despite the great methodological contribution of the New Archaeology, many of the central concerns of the pre-New Archaeology era need to be rediscovered if an adequate *archaeological* discussion is to take place. Of course, the traditional approaches themselves had flaws, and these have to be dealt with. But the older approaches do not have to be thrown out totally, in the way that the New Archaeology sometimes rejected 'normative' archaeology (Flannery 1967; Binford 1962; 1965).

My own route to this viewpoint was substantially drawn by the ethnoarchaeological fieldwork reported in *Symbols in Action* (1982a). The three main ideas which developed out of that work, all of which have parallels in pre-New Archaeology, were (1) that material culture was meaningfully constituted, (2) that the individual needed to be a part of theories of material culture and social change, and (3) that despite the independent existence of archaeology, its closest ties were with history. I wish now to summarize these three 'problems'.

Cultural meanings and context

Schiffer (1976) has already argued that cultural transforms affect the relationship between material residues and the behaviour of the people who produced them. *Symbols in Action* showed further the importance of these 'c-transforms', as Schiffer called them.

At first sight such realization offers no threat to archaeology as a generalizing scientific discipline. Schiffer showed how one could generalize about c-transforms. For example, it can be shown that as the duration and intensity of use of a site increase, so there is more organization and secondary movement of refuse away from activity areas. In my work in Baringo it became clear that material culture was often *not* a direct reflection of human behaviour; rather it was a transformation of that behaviour.

For example, it had earlier been suggested that the stylistic similarity between objects increased as interaction between people increased. In fact, at the borders between ethnic groups in Baringo, the more interaction between people, the less the stylistic similarity. But, again, such findings can be incorporated within New Archaeology because it is possible to generalize and state the 'law' that material culture distinctiveness is correlated with the degree of negative reciprocity between groups (Hodder 1979). So the more competition between groups the more marked the material culture boundaries between them.

Another case in which it became clear that material culture was neither a simple nor a direct reflection of human behaviour was burial. Binford (1971) had suggested a general correlation between the complexity of mortuary ceremonialism and the complexity of social organization. As Parker Pearson (1982) elegantly showed, in a study of modern and recent burial practices in Cambridge, such generalizations failed to take into account the cultural transformation of the relationship between burials and people. Even a highly differentiated society of the type found in Cambridge today might choose to bury its dead in an 'egalitarian' fashion.

Once again such work does not necessarily result in the final spanner being thrown in the works of New Archaeology. It might be possible to find some law-like generalizations about why societies represent and express themselves differently in burial customs. For example, at early stages in the development of a more highly ranked society, social status might be exaggerated and 'naturalized' in death, while at later stages the social ranking might be 'denied' in burial variability.

But in the case of burial practices, such generalizations are unconvincing and the force of the notion that material culture is an *indirect* reflection of human society becomes clear. Here we begin to see that it is ideas, beliefs and meanings which interpose themselves between people and things. How burial reflects society clearly depends on attitudes to death.

Much the same can be said of cultural boundaries and refuse deposition. Whether a particular artifact type does or does not express the boundary of an ethnic group depends on the ideas people in that society have about different artifacts and what is an appropriate artifact for ethnic group marking. The relationship between refuse and social organization depends on attitudes to dirt. Thus even short-term camps may have highly organized rubbish and long-term camps may allow refuse build-up of a type that we today would find abhorrent and unhygienic.

These cultural attitudes and meanings about material culture seemed to frustrate the generalizing aims of the New Archaeology, since all material culture could now be seen to be meaningfully constituted. In this way there is all the difference in the world between a consideration of symbolism in archaeology and its sibling 'symbolic anthropology'. The latter can remain as a subset within anthropology, alongside economic anthropology, and so on. It can be argued that economic anthropology is studied without recourse to symbolic anthropology. But in archaeology *all* inference is via material culture. If material culture, all of it, has a symbolic dimension such that the relationship between people and things is affected, then *all* of archaeology, economic and social, is implicated.

The problem then becomes, not 'how do we study symbolism in the past?', but 'how do we do archaeology at all?'.

Within New Archaeology the methodology to be employed in interpreting the past was 'hard' and universal. Simplistically put, one could correlate material culture patterning with human patterning, and 'read off' the latter from the former by applying general laws and Middle Range Theory. Ultimately material culture could be seen as the product of adaptation with the environment, both physical and social. So, if one kept asking *why* the material culture patterning is as it is, one was always taken back to questions of material survival. With such a 'reductionist' approach one can always predict what the material culture means, what it reflects, in any environmental context.

But to claim that culture is meaningfully constituted is ultimately to claim that aspects of culture are *irreducible*. The relationship between material culture and human organization is partly social, as we shall see below. But it is also dependent on a set of cultural attitudes which cannot be predicted from or reduced to an environment. The cultural relationships are not caused by anything else outside themselves. They just are. The task of archaeologists is to interpret this irreducible component of culture so that the society behind the material evidence can be 'read'.

How does one go about such 'reading'? It is often claimed that material objects are mute, that they do not speak, so how can one understand them? Certainly an object from the past does not say anything of itself. Handed an object from an unknown culture archaeologists will often have difficulties in providing an interpretation. But to look at objects by themselves is really not archaeology at all. Archaeology is concerned with finding objects in layers and other contexts (rooms, sites, pits, burials) so that their date and meaning can be interpreted.

As soon as the context of an object is known it is no longer totally mute. Clues as to its meaning are given by its context. Artifacts are found in graves around the necks of the skeletons and are interpreted as necklaces. Objects found in elaborate non-settlement contexts are termed ritual. Clearly we cannot claim that, even in context, objects tell us their cultural meaning, but on the other hand they are not totally mute. The interpretation of meaning is constrained by the interpretation of context.

In *Symbols in Action*, the emphasis on context led to discussion of burial, style, exchange, refuse discard, settlement organization. All these realms of material culture could now be seen as different contexts in relation to each other. Artifacts might mean different things in these different contexts, but the meanings from one realm might be related, in a distorted way, to the meanings in other realms. The 'reading' of the archaeological record had to take such cultural transformations into account.

A number of problems and questions arose from such a viewpoint. First, what *is* the context? Context itself has to be interpreted in the data, and the definition of context is a matter for debate. Is the context of a particular artifact type found in cemeteries a part of the body, the grave, a group of graves, the cemetery, the region, or what? How does one decide on the boundary which defines the context?

Second, even assuming we can construct meanings from contextual associations, similarities and differences, are these cultural meanings in people's minds? Certainly much of the cultural meaning of material objects is not conscious. Few of us are aware of the full range of reasons which lead us to choose a particular item of dress as appropriate for a given context. But do we need to get at the conscious and subconscious meanings in people's minds, or are there simply cultural rules and practices which can be observed from the outside? Do we simply have to describe the unconscious cultural rules of a society or do we have to get at people's perceptions of those rules? For example, is it enough to say that in a particular cultural tradition burial variability correlates with social variability or that burial is organized by a culture/nature transform, or do we need to understand people's attitudes to death, getting 'inside their minds'?

The third question has already been touched upon. To what extent can we generalize about ideas in people's minds? Certain general principles concerning the relationships between structural oppositions, associations, similarities, contexts and meanings are used in interpreting the past and the world around us today. Even the notion that meaning derives from contextual associations is a general theory. To what extent are such generalizations valid? And further, what is the aim of archaeology? Is it to provide generalizations? If we say that meanings are context dependent, then all we can do is come to an understanding of each cultural context in its own right, as a unique set of cultural dispositions and practices. We cannot generalize from one culture to another. Even if there are some general propositions we need to use in interpreting the past, these are, by their very general nature, trivial – hardly the focus for scientific enquiry. To what extent can we generalize about unique cultural contexts, and why should we want to generalize in any case?

These questions are also relevant in relation to the second problem that derived from *Symbols in Action*.

The active individual

Material culture does not just exist. It is made by someone. It is produced to do something. Therefore it does not passively *reflect* society – rather, it creates society through the actions of individuals.

The question of the importance of the individual in society is an old one. On the one hand we have John Donne's famous words, 'No man is an island, entire of itself, every man is a piece of the continent, a part of the main.' This is an aspect of the truth, that we need to see how society affects the individual. Ultimately this view says that individuals are of little significance in the tide of human history. On the other hand J. S. Mill, a classical individualist, said 'Men are not, when brought together, converted into another kind of substance.'

In the New Archaeology, the individual was avoided, argued out of social theory. As Flannery noted (1967), the aim was not to reach the individual Indian behind the artifact, but the system behind both Indian and artifact. It is argued by the processual school in archaeology that there are systems so basic in nature that culture and individuals are powerless to divert them. This is a trend towards determinism – theory building is seen as being concerned with discovering deterministic causal relationships. There is a close link here between discarding notions of cultural belief and of the individual. Both are seen as being unassailable through archaeological evidence, and both are unpredictable and inhibit generalization.

Yet the notion that archaeology cannot 'see' individuals is deceptive. It is true that archaeologists can rarely know the names of those who made pots, or the names of great leaders of society. By emphasizing the individual in social theory I do not mean to suggest that we should identify 'great men' and 'great women'; but each archaeological object is produced by an individual (or a group of individuals), not by a social system. Each pot is made by an individual person forming the shape, inscribing the design. Archaeology thus raises in an acute form the problem of the relationship between the individual and society. What is the relationship between the individual pot and the society as a whole?

Within the New Archaeology this central question was simply bypassed. Individual pots were examined solely as passive reflections of the socio-cultural system. Each pot, each artifact could be examined to see how it functioned for the system as a whole. For example, the pot reflected status and thus helped to regulate the flow of energy and resources within the system. In addition, the system was seen as developing 'over the long term'. Thus individual instances of variability which did not act for the good of the system as a whole would be of no significance for the long-term survival of the system and would in any case hardly be visible archaeologically.

These two notions – the overall adaptive system and the long term – led to a rejection of the individual in archaeological theory. As a result, material culture became a passive reflection of the social system. Whatever individuals had in their heads when they made a pot, the only thing that was important was how that pot functioned in the social system. What the individual was trying to do with the object became irrelevant.

The ethnographic work reported in *Symbols in Action* showed the inadequacy of this view. For example, in a Lozi village, pottery similarities did not passively reflect learning networks and interaction frequency. Rather the pottery style was used to create social differences and allegiances within the village; it was produced to have an active role. Similarly, some artifacts indicate social boundaries in Baringo, in Kenya, but spears, for example, do not. This is because spear styles are used by young men to disrupt the authority of older men. They play an active role.

That material culture can act back and affect the society and behaviour which produced it can readily be accepted within processual archaeology (Rathje 1978, p. 52). In particular, town and house architecture clearly channels and acts upon later behaviour. On the other hand, material culture cannot of itself do anything: if it does 'act back' on society it must do so within the frameworks of meaning within the society itself. The way in which material culture acts on people is social; the action can only exist within a social framework of beliefs, concepts and dispositions.

Material culture and its associated meanings are played out as parts of social strategies. Individuals do not fill predetermined roles, acting out their scripts. If they did, there would be little need for the active use of material culture in order to negotiate social position and create social change. We are not simply pawns in a game, determined by a system – rather, we use a myriad of means, including material culture symbolism, to create new roles, to redefine existing ones and to deny the existence of others.

It could be argued that processual archaeology is indeed concerned with individual variability. After all, did it not react against normative approaches and emphasize the importance of situational adaptive behaviour? The question of whether processual archaeology escaped a normative position will be discussed throughout this volume. For the moment it is necessary to set the scene by clarifying some of the meanings given to the term normative in archaeology. First, it is often used to refer to the culture-historical approach. In this context it sometimes has pejorative connotations; it refers to descriptive culture history. This is not the sense in which I will use the term in this volume. Second, 'normative' refers to the notion that culture is made up of a set of shared beliefs. The implication is sometimes present that the shared ideas (the norms) hinder situational variability. Third, there is a prescriptive component to norms – they indicate what should be done. In this sense norms refer to rules of behaviour. Of course one can be critical of the normative approach (in the first sense) while still being interested in norms in the second and third senses, but both these latter meanings of the word give little in the way of a role to individuals as social actors. A more general critique of normative positions will be required in this volume.

Historical context

In the reaction against culture history and normative archaeology, processual archaeologists turned to anthropology. Ultimately the main reason why the New Archaeology never really took hold in Europe to the extent that it did in America may be that in Europe archaeology is intellectually and administratively (in universities) closely linked to history, not anthropology. In American processual archaeology, the new approach was to be cross-cultural, looking at systems in relation to their environments and producing universal statements. In effect a timeless past was produced. System trajectories were examined, but time was sliced into segments and attention was focussed on the cross-cultural regularities in changes from type *a* to type *b* (for example from mobile hunter–gatherers to settled farmers).

While the discussion so far in this chapter has implied that cross-cultural laws which are more than trivial are unlikely to exist, what is the possibility of historical laws – that is generalizations valid through time in a particular context? Since action in the world partly depends on concepts, and since concepts are learnt through experience in the world, in which one is brought up and lives, it is feasible that long-term continuities in cultural traditions exist, continually being renegotiated and transformed, but nevertheless generated from within. Part of the aim of archaeology may be to identify whether such long-term continuities exist, and how they are transformed and changed.

It was noted earlier that an emphasis on cultural meanings is here taken to imply that culture is not reducible to material effects. In explaining why a cultural form has a specific meaning and use, it is necessary to examine its previous associations and contexts, its diffusion and sequence. While diffusion and cultural continuity are social processes, the pre-existing cultural form also influences what comes after. This is because human beings can only perceive and act through a cultural medium which they both create and live within. As Childe (1936) put it, man creates traditions, but traditions make the man – man makes himself.

It might be thought that there is a danger here of a new type of reductionism. Rather than reducing cultural behaviour to survival, there is the possibility of an infinite regress as cultural forms are interpreted in terms of previous cultural forms, backwards until we get to the first stone-tool ever made, in the temporal mists of the Palaeolithic. While it will rarely be necessary to go to such historical lengths, it is difficult to see why one should want to deny the importance of culture-historical work. There is something in all of us of the decisions made in the flaking of the very first hand-axe. Only archaeology can achieve this grand design. But even when we get to the origin of some idea it is not reduced to something outside itself. The cultural form remains created, specific and irreducible.

While it may ultimately be desirable to trace the creation of the present out of the distant past, the transformations of meaning over such time periods are considerable. More frequently we can gain adequate insight into cultural meanings by examining the more immediate historical context.

It *is* important, therefore, to examine where things come from. This was the focus of culture history within traditional archaeology. We now have to see the diffusion of traits as a social and meaningful process; the associations of an item in another or in a previous cultural context affect the use of that item within a new context. Diffusion is thus explanatory, not descriptive, as is so often claimed.

While it is argued that archaeology should reassert its European ties with history, it is also important to see the differences between archaeology and history. To the extent that historical explanation can be defined by its reference to antecedent contexts and events (an inadequate or incomplete description, as I will argue in chapter 5), archaeology is part of history. Yet archaeology is about material culture not documents. The writing of ink on paper is itself one type of material culture, and the inference of meaning from such evidence is equivalent to that for material objects in general. In this sense, history is part of archaeology. Even though historical documents contain considerably more contextual information when we recognize the language they are written in, the process of inference is still one of giving meaning to the past material world.

Conclusion

In the course of this volume I hope to discuss the problems raised in this first chapter. The aim is to meet the challenges posed to archaeology by a recognition of the importance of cultural meaning, the active individual and history. In summary, we can see that such recognition has effects in the three central areas of archaeological debate. These are (1) the relationship between material culture and society – how material culture relates to people, (2) the causes of change – what causes social, economic and cultural change, and (3) epistemology and inference – how archaeologists interpret the past.

1 Behaviour–material culture

It has always been recognized that the relationship between behaviour and material culture is the central difficulty to be resolved in archaeology. The problems in this relationship were early recognized in the only partial correspondences discovered between material 'cultures' and 'peoples' (Childe 1951).

The contribution of processual archaeology was an attempt to think systematically about the relationship between behaviour and material culture. In much early work the dominant theme was: behaviour → material culture. Material culture was the passive by-product of human behaviour. This view is seen in the matrilocal residence hypothesis (Longacre 1970) and in theories about the relationship between population and settlement area (Naroll 1962) and between style and interaction (Plog 1978). The attempt by Binford (1983) to identify Middle Range Theory, insofar as this can be applied to cultural processes, recaptures the same desire for secure, unambiguous relationships, essentially equivalent to Schiffer's (1976) laws, between material culture and human behaviour. More recently, as was shown above, this cross-cultural approach has been extended (Rathje 1978) to include the notion that material culture acts back upon society, forming a two-way relationship: behaviour ←→ material culture.

In this book I wish to go further and argue that the relationship between behaviour and material culture depends on the actions of individuals within particular culture-historical contexts.

behaviour ←→ material culture
↑
individual,
culture,
history

There is thus no direct, universal cross-cultural relationship between behaviour and material culture. Frameworks of meaning intervene and these have to be interpreted by the archaeologist. This endeavour must be undertaken by all of those who want to examine the past as archaeologists, even if we are mainly interested in economics and social organization rather than symbolism. Even if I want to say that the economy at a particular site was based on hunting many wild animals because of the high percentage of wild animal bones on the site, I need to make some assumptions about attitudes to animals, bones, and waste or dirt. For example, I need to assume that people ate, or discarded the residues from the animals they ate, on sites (rather than eating and discarding off sites, throwing bones in rivers where they would not survive archaeologically, or burning the bones to ash). Whatever I want to say about human behaviour in the past, cultural meanings need to be assumed.

2 Cause–effect

The second major area of research is the causes of social change. Again, simple notions of cause → effect (technological change leads to population increase, for example) have been replaced by cause ←→ effect relationships through the introduction of systems, feedback loops, multiplier effects and multiple causality. Most archaeologists today would accept that the causes of social change are complex, involving many different factors – economic, social and ideological – and there have recently been many interesting attempts to relate these factors into complex interlocking systems (chapter 2).

Within such work, however, there remains the notion that causes have effects which are to some degree universal and predictable. On the other hand, the central importance of the individual perception of causes leads to a different view.

$$\text{cause} \longleftrightarrow \text{effect}$$
$$\uparrow$$
$$\text{individual,}$$
$$\text{culture,}$$
$$\text{history}$$

Causes in the form of events, conditions and consequences (intended and unintended) in the world, cannot have social effects except via human perception and evaluation of them. Thus land erosion may be a *cause* with the *effect* that people abandon their village and disperse. But the fact of land erosion does not by itself determine any particular response because there are many ways of dealing with or avoiding or preventing land erosion. How land erosion or its effects are perceived, and how the possible responses are evaluated, depend on how land erosion is involved in individual social strategies within particular culture-historical contexts.

This is saying more than that ideology is important in human adaptation and that it functions in various ways. Within most archaeological discussion of ideology, the belief system is seen as a predictable response of the adaptive system (chapter 2); it is claimed here, however, that the particular content of the values and traditions that are constructed within historical channels is the medium through which adaptation occurs. Thus causes (social or physical) do not have social effects; rather, an historical tradition reproduces itself in relation to events in the world.

3 Fact–theory

Through much of the early development of archaeology an empiricist stance was maintained, in which the facts were seen to speak for themselves – 'let the pots speak'. Thus Colt Hoare said that we speak from facts not theory. It was held that by staying close to the facts certain things, though by no means all things, could be known with security. As we shall see later, this is a simplification of a complex set of beliefs held by archaeologists prior to the emergence of processual archaeology. But in general, inference could be seen as following the design: data → theory.

More recently an alternative view has been emphasized, in which data are collected in relation to a theory. The hypothetico-deductive approach involved deducing from a theory various implications, and testing these implications against the data. Binford's (1967) smudge-pit example provides a good illustration of this procedure. Renfrew (1982) has depicted the relationship between theory and data as data ⟷ theory. Fact and theory confront each other but each changes in relation to the other.

Binford and Sabloff (1982) have in fact suggested that the relationship between theory and data is so close that data are observed within theory, and that therefore observational data are really theories (in Binford and Sabloff's terms the observational data are paradigm dependent). Thus, while all the approaches mentioned above would argue that the real world exists separate from our observations of it, more and more of the observational process is seen as being theory dependent. The bare bones that are left are the facts in the real world which we can never observe.

The problems of observation raised by post-positivist philosophy can be exemplified in the diagrams shown in Fig. 1. Before we can measure and compare such objects we have to decide what they are. For example, if we decide to measure the front faces of all such boxes, which is the front face? Or if we decide to measure the distance between the lower and upper beaks of all such birds, we have to be able to differentiate between birds and deer.

Such problems are particularly acute in the study of prehistoric art, but they pose a major difficulty for all archaeology

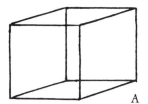

Fig. 1. The relationship between data and theory. (A) Which is the front edge of the box? (B) A bird looking up or a deer looking down? (C) A bear climbing a tree or just a gnarled trunk?

since before one can measure or count, compare or contrast, one has to form categories (types of pots, contexts, cultures and so on). These categories are formed through the process of perception.

The solution followed by Binford and Sabloff (1982) is to invoke Middle Range Theory. They argue that independent instruments of measurement can be brought in to test the relationship between material culture and the society which produced it, and that in this way one can 'objectively' test between paradigms. This answer is inadequate (a) because what one measures depends on perception and categorization, and (b) because there can be no *independent* instruments of measurement since methodology is itself theory dependent.

Although it will be argued in this volume that the real world does constrain what we can say about it, it is also clear that the concept of 'data' involves both the real world and our theories about it. As a result, the theories one espouses about the past depend very much on one's own social and cultural context. Trigger (1980), Leone (1978) and others have shown with great effect how changing interpretations of the past depend on changing social and cultural contexts in the present. Individuals within society today use the past within social strategies. In other words, the data–theory relationship is conceived and manipulated within cultural and historical contexts.

$$\text{Fact} \longleftrightarrow \text{theory}$$
$$\uparrow$$
$$\text{individual,}$$
$$\text{culture,}$$
$$\text{history}$$

Towards the end of this volume I wish to examine the varied implications of the realization that there can be no 'testing' of theory against data, no independent measuring devices and no secure knowledge about the past. It seems to me that most archaeologists have shied away from these problems since at first sight they seem destructive: the whole fabric of archaeology as a scientific discipline, accepted since the early development of archaeology, is threatened. I wish to argue that the problems need to be faced if archaeology is to remain a rigorous discipline and if archaeologists are to be socially responsible.

2 The systems approach

In chapter 1 the question was posed: how do we infer cultural meanings in material remains from the past? In this and the following chapters various approaches to achieving this end will be discussed. The search is for an approach that takes adequate account of the active individual in an historical and cultural context.

It is necessary first to make a distinction between two broad classes of approach followed by archaeologists, which I shall term materialist and idealist. We shall see later that these terms have numerous senses within different schools of thought; for the moment I wish to give them provisional but precise meanings.

For Kohl (1981, p. 89) materialism 'accords greater causal weight to a society's behaviour than to its thoughts, reflections, or justifications for its behaviour'. This definition needs to be extended to include the nature of inference within materialist approaches. In this book I mean by materialist approaches those that infer cultural meanings from the relationships between people and their environment. Within such a framework the ideas in people's minds can be predicted from their economy, technology, social and material production. Given a way of organizing matter and energy, an appropriate ideological framework can be predicted. According to this view, we do not need to see inside people's minds, because we can predict their ideology from the 'materialistic' evidence available to archaeology.

By idealist I mean any approach which accepts that there is some component of human action which is not predictable from a material base, but which comes from the human mind or from culture in some sense. In chapter 1, I referred to the viewpoint that culture was not entirely reducible to other variables, that to some extent culture is what culture is. In inferring cultural meanings in the past, there is no necessary relationship between social and material organization of resources on the one hand and cultural ideas and values on the other.

The distinction made above is equivalent to Gellner's (1982) identification of 'covering law' and 'emanationist' conceptions of causation. The former limits itself to the world of experience and seeks causality in the pattern of similar experiences, the regular associations, the observed laws; the latter, on the other hand, postulates inner essences, normally hidden from view, which lie behind and bind together visible phenomena.

In this chapter I wish to examine a common recent approach to recovering past cultural meanings, which in my view is often materialist, and 'covering law' in nature – the use of systemic adaptive theory. Kohl (1981, p. 95) argues that there is no necessary relationship between materialism and systems analysis. In practice, however, systems analysis has been the vehicle for the application of models emphasizing ecology and economy, based on predictable law-like relationships. I intend to illustrate these points by taking a number of representative examples. It must be emphasized that these examples are chosen precisely because they are good examples within the framework used. In criticizing them I do not criticize the authors and their work, only the framework which they have adopted.

The article by Sherratt (1982) on changes in economy and society in the East Hungarian plain between the 6th and 4th millenia B.C., is the first example of the way in which systemic approaches have begun to incorporate the ideational sub-system, including style and ritual. Randsborg (1982) also shows the way ideologies, particularly attitudes to death, change through time in relation to other sub-systems. He examines sequences of change, related to climatic variation in Denmark between the Bronze Age and the Viking period.

Much recent work on symbolism and style has as its starting point an article by Wobst (1977). This important and creative work shows the way in which style can be linked to processes of information exchange, and Wobst relates the information exchange sub-system to flows of matter and energy. Wobst explains style by its functioning in relation to other variables, and I will therefore describe his approach as systemic.

An equally important and influential article is that by Flannery and Marcus (1976) in which ideology is seen to play a part in regulating the social and economic sub-systems throughout long periods in the Oaxaca valley, Mexico. They show the way in which the Zapotec cosmology can be seen as a means of organizing information about the world.

A materialist approach to culture?

The first point that is suggested by comparing these articles is that they are all materialist in the sense outlined above. They all see style, symbolism, ideology and cultural meaning as conferring adaptive advantage. If pushed, all will *reduce* culture to survival. Thus, Sherratt starts by pointing out that the well-watered East Hungarian plains are a natural breeding ground for cattle. In the 5th millenium B.C. settlement expanded into the surrounding uplands where people had access to flint and obsidian. Lowland cattle resources were therefore traded for upland resources, and this regional exchange led to intensification of production (of cattle for example). People agglomerated into larger, more permanent and defended sites in order to handle and protect a valuable and mobile resource (cattle). This led to changes in the styles of pottery decoration which became more diverse, elaborate and localized since 'it was advantageous to make local products sufficiently distinctive to break into the flourishing regional exchange system'. Ritual also changed because the competition over resources led to the need for closer control *within* groups, which was achieved by ritual and ideological means. There was an elaboration of cult objects, figurines and so on.

Typically then, we move from environment and economy to society and settlement, to ritual and ideology, predicting the functions upwards from the material basis. The same pattern is seen in Randsborg's example. He notes a relationship through time between the following: (a) optimal climate, expansion of settlement and richness of burial goods. This correlation is seen to be the result of less strict 'norms' of inheritance over mobile wealth. In periods of good climate and expansion, there are less fixed successional, inheritance rules: succession is challenged and there is competition at death. As a result valued goods are placed in graves as part of the rivalry over succession. (b) In periods of contraction of settlement in sub-optimal weather conditions there is intensification of production and poor graves, even though social stratification is still evident in other spheres such as hoards. From climate, economy and society, Randsborg predicts a set of attitudes to death and burial.

Wobst clearly states that he is concerned not with the production of artifacts but with their use lives. He is concerned with the adaptive advantage that artifacts provide in information exchange. 'Learned behaviour and symbolizing ability greatly increase the capacity of human operators to interact with their environment through the medium of artifacts. This capacity . . . improves their ability to harness and process energy and matter' (p. 320). In looking at the adaptive advantages style may convey, Wobst suggests a number of cross-cultural generalizations. For example, artifact style gains in value if the potential receivership is neither too close socially (since emitter and receiver will be acquainted) nor too distant (since decoding of the message is unreliable). Thus, as the size of social units increases so that there is more interaction with socially intermediate receivers, artifact stylistic behaviour will increase. Another generalization is that 'the less an artifact is visible to members of a given group, the less appropriate it is to carry stylistic messages of any kind' (p. 328).

Such work concentrates on material functions and reduces symbolic behaviour to utility and adaptation. General statements are derived suggesting predictable relationships between economy and society: for example I have suggested (1979) that material culture boundaries are more marked where there is increased negative reciprocity between groups. In the same vein Wobst suggests in relation to Yugoslavian folk costume that 'in areas of strong inter-group competition one would expect a higher proportion of people wearing hats that signal group affiliation than in areas with relatively stable homogeneous populations' (p. 333).

Flannery and Marcus (1976) suggest a broader context for such generalizations. They show the way symbolism and ritual can be seen as part of human ecology, following the ecological stance of Rappaport (1971). Their concern is with the way ritual regulates the relationship between people and environment; the Zapotec cosmology is seen as a way of giving order to and regulating natural events. Ritual blood-letting, using sting-ray spines, shows to other members of a community that a farmer is making a loss and needs the support of gifts of maize. Human ecosystems involve the exchange of matter, energy and information.

To what extent can these materialist systemic approaches explain cultural meaning, ideology and ritual? The first point to be made is that they are not intended to explain the 'becoming' of cultural production. As Wobst clearly states, his interest is in the use and functions of artifact styles, not their production. This is a difficulty of all functional, adaptive explanations, where the 'cause' of an event is also its 'effect'. Thus in explaining how something like sting-ray spine bloodletting came about, we refer to a later effect, the regulation of resources. This temporal inversion is, however, recognized by most systems theorists, and answered by saying that archaeologists can only look at adaptive advantage over the long term, at what is selected for survival. Within this view there is little concern with why something was produced.

Thus, almost by definition, most of the cultural variability dug up by archaeologists is ruled out of the court of explanation. We cannot explain why a string-ray spine is used, why blood-letting is used rather than other artifacts and rituals. Reference is made only to gross characteristics of cultural behaviour – Sherratt's more elaborate pottery and ritual, Randsborg's richness of burial goods, Wobst's increases and decreases of stylistic behaviour. In most cases we cannot explain why a particular ritual, or why a ritual at all, are used for a particular function, since other things could presumably have done the same job equally well. The difficulty is made clear if we start, not from the adaptive functional end, but from the decoration, the particular squiggle painted on a pot. We can hardly say that squiggles on pots are determined by adaptive advantage. There is a poverty to systemic arguments which do not allow us to explain specific cultural variability. A great amount is left unaccounted for.

How are the ideational meanings assigned in these studies? Is the imputation of meaning achieved critically? Many archaeologists retain an empiricist view and are sceptical of the ideational realm, which is often equated with the speculative and non-scientific, and prefer to talk of material functions rather than ideas which were in people's minds in the past. However, in my view it is impossible to discuss function to the exclusion of the ideational realm, for at least three reasons.

First, the notion of 'function' assumes some 'end', or several 'ends' which are in some way ranked in order of importance. For example, if one is discussing whether barbed or unbarbed points are more efficient in fulfilling their function(s), one has also to discuss what these functions were, and their relative importance. Such 'ends' might be to wound or kill a person or animal, from near or far, quickly or slowly, with or without the possibility of reuse of the same implement, and so on. And of course the implement may have important symbolic meanings which could affect its use and killing potential. These various 'ends' are produced within a matrix of cultural meanings.

Second, before we can talk of the functions of an object we normally produce categories of object – points, barbed points, pots, and so on. We then compare and contrast the functions of these different categories. The system of categorization we choose will partly depend on its functions, but it will also involve a considerable degree of subjectivity. We decide, often by convention, what is a meaningful category.

Third, the hypothesis concerning function is always based on an assumption about the meaning of an object. Even to call an object an axe is to assume that people in the past saw it in the same light as we do today – as an object used to cut down trees. Function and meaning are inextricably linked; this is particularly clear when we discuss the social functions of objects. Such social functions depend on a conceptual meaning which we often impose covertly and uncritically.

For example, Randsborg suggests that burial is used for social display in certain social and environmental conditions. Given challenged norms of succession it is implied that burials will be part of status rivalry. There is no attempt to understand whether attitudes to death really do relate to such considerations in Denmark. Presumably the burials could have had quite other meanings. To say that burial richness equals social rivalry we have to 'think ourselves into' the prehistoric attitudes to burials. Also, in periods of poor climate in the Danish sequence there are poor graves, yet Randsborg shows that hoards are rich and varied in these periods. It is conceivable that these hoards were deposited in bogs at death, and are equivalent to the grave furnishings in periods of optimal climate. The hoards may have had the same meaning, and hence the same function as the burials. Without getting at these cultural meanings we cannot get at how the items functioned. As a further example of this point we can return to Wobst's Yugoslavian head-dresses. He uses these to support the general statement that more visible cultural items carry messages to larger social units – the head-gear is highly visible. But there are many visible ways of using the body to show social group allegiance at a distance, particularly, for example, posture, trousers, coats etc. Wobst may be correct in his reconstruction, but if he is it is because he has correctly hypothesized the indigenous perceptions concerning which aspects of the body are important in marking social affiliation. The head-dress may be highly visible but it may not have been perceived as highly visible, or it may have been perceived to have meanings not primarily related to identity display.

I have made (1984a) a related point about the megaliths of Europe. These monumental burial mounds have been widely accepted as territorial or group markers (Renfrew 1976), legitimating competition over resources by reference to the ancestors. Now while this may seem perfectly reasonable, it is important to recognize that the theory about the social functions (competition, legitimation) is based on a theory about what the tombs meant (ancestors, the past). Clearly, they *could* have been perceived in a different way, in which case their social function might have been different. An apparently materialist, covering law argument is based on the imputation of perceptions inside the culture. A similar point can be made about the archaeological identification of 'prestige' items.

Within the covering law, systemic approach, cultural meanings are imposed, but always from the outside, without adequate consideration. The assignment of cultural meanings is normally based on Western attitudes, which are implicit and undiscussed. It is assumed that burials, rituals, head-gear and pot decoration have universal social functions, linked to their universal meanings; objects are wrenched out of their context and explained cross-culturally.

The partition of cultural systems into various sub-systems, which is the starting point for all systemic analyses, is itself based on a Western view of the world. The divisions made between subsistence, trade, society, symbolism may not be appropriate for past societies. The division, based itself on a covering law, may appear to give equal weight to all the sub-systems, but in practice, as we have seen, the 'material' sub-systems are given dominance. Flannery and Marcus try to give a more important role to ideology, arguing that systems must be seen to work *within* a cosmology, bracketed by and organized by a set of cultural beliefs. But even here the ideology has a passive regulative role, working for the good of the system as a whole, and over the long term. Any systems analysis involves making assumptions about cultural meanings, and we have seen that in archaeology these assumptions are often materialist in character.

The passive individual

As a result of the passive view of ideology within most systems analyses, individuals play little part in the theories – they only appear as predictable automata, driven by covering laws. In the examples discussed, individuals appear controlled by rituals according to universal expectations; there is no sense in which they actively manipulate and negotiate ideologies.

This point is evident in relation to style. Wobst concentrates on style and information exchange: the only thing that matters is whether a message is emitted and received efficiently. Certainly the organization of information as studied by Wobst could be said to be active in that the information aids the organization of energy and resources, but since there is no interest in such work in the production of style, one is left with the impression that individuals are situated passively in pre-existing roles and that the material symbols simply allow such roles to be organized efficiently. There is little idea here that individuals have to create roles in action and in the competent manipulation of the symbolic world – one has the impression that 'other things being equal' it is simply a matter of following the rules. The active individual plays a minor part in such theories.

Another aspect of the systemic approach to ideology is that individuals appear to be easily fooled. They are easily duped by the dominant ideology, and they easily accept the legitimation of control. In Sherratt's example, rituals appear which legitimate control within groups. Presumably everybody is duped by, or at least accepts, the new ideology without being able to penetrate its raison d'être.

It is perhaps surprising that, although the whole of the New Archaeology or processual archaeology was based on the rejection of normative archaeology, the systemic covering law approach is itself normative, in the sense that the beliefs and rituals, the meaning of style, are all rules shared by members of social communities. There is no indication that different people or sub-sections in society might view the same thing (a ritual such as blood-letting, or burial display) differently. Wobst in particular discusses the way in which style allows members of a group to evaluate how closely a given individual is subscribing to the behavioural norms of the group. Headdresses are seen as having a common significance throughout the society in which they are worn.

History and time

If, within the systems approach, each society has a set of norms which regulate relationships with the environment, how does social change occur? The way in which time is treated is distinctive. Cultural development is broken up into temporal phases, and adaptation with the environment is assessed for each phase separately. The trajectory of the system is subdivided and then put back together again in order to see general developments through time. This division into periods is particularly clearly seen in Sherratt's and Randsborg's work where each phase has a different climatic, environmental, subsistence orientation and is treated separately. Even if the new environmental context is based on the old (as when settlement expansion is necessary after earlier land infill), explanation of each phase is undertaken separately applying covering laws.

The difficulty thus becomes one of explaining the move from phase *a* to phase *b*. This may be done by arguing for a new environmental, economic context necessitating social and ideological change, or by arguing for internal problems and pathologies leading to change, but it is unclear how a *particular* resolution to the new problems is found. Of all the choices available, including retraction and stability as opposed to growth, how is one choice made? Systems theory in archaeology has been concerned to examine the functions of things which already exist. By disregarding production, creation and innovation, by only looking at the adaptive qualities of a system, we cannot explain how that system developed; neither can we explain how people come to accept the new system. How did the new ideational system, the social legitimation come about? Where did the new system of beliefs come from and why did people accept them?

In order to explain system change, it thus becomes necessary to see how phase *b* is generated out of phase *a*. If we can understand the ideological structures in phase *a*, then we can begin to examine how the change to phase *b* was produced and given meaning. Our analysis of systemic change must thus take historical meanings into account. The choices about system trajectory are formulated within a pre-existing but changing cultural framework. The systemic analysis which most closely meets these requirements is that of Flannery and Marcus, who achieve an interpretation which, despite the shortcomings mentioned above, has many contextual components. The Zapotec cosmology is understood as being unique and historically particular. Rather than imposing modern Western notions of satisfying or maximizing strategies, Flannery and Marcus suggest the Zapotec had a 'harmonizing ethic' in which a particular relationship with the cosmos underlay ritual, society and economy.

> The Zapotec world was an orderly place in which human actions were based on empirical observations, interpreted in the light of a coherent body of logic. Once that logic is understood, all Zapotec behaviour – whether economic political or religious – makes sense as a series of related and internally consistent responses based on the same set of underlying principles. In other words, one very non-Western metaphysic regulated exchanges of matter, energy and information. (p. 383)

While this view is highly normative, it certainly defines a framework within which social and economic change can be explained and understood. The Zapotec metaphysic is the medium for social change in relation to a changing human and physical environment.

Measuring and predicting mind

Flannery and Marcus derive the Zapotec metaphysic from historical and ethnographic sources. How is this to be done for prehistoric societies for which there is no cultural continuity into the present? As implied by Gellner's description of the covering law approach, the methods most closely linked to systems archaeology are modelled on the natural sciences. Ritual, social organization and ideology are seen as having universal cross-cultural relationships with the material, observable world; we can therefore infer the ideology from measurable archaeological data, and we can do this with security.

This point is made forcefully by Renfrew (1983a) in his lecture 'Towards an Archaeology of Mind'. Here he suggests that archaeologists can only get at meaning insofar as the meaning has effects on the social world and on artifact patterning. Meaning here is separated from material culture in a fact ↔ theory opposition. Renfrew wants to infer cognitive processes without dizzy intuitive leaps; to achieve this it is necessary to develop explicit procedures and a coherent body of theory so that inferences can be made securely.

Such a direction appears to imply that there are some universal measurements of mind. The natural science model is clear, but the internal tension within this view is distinctive. On the one hand, Renfrew, here, and Binford and Sabloff (1982), argue for independent yardsticks for measuring the past; on the other hand they accept that the past is perceived within our own social and cultural matrix. Renfrew also claims, in line with Flannery and Marcus, that 'each culture has its own "helix of interaction", its own historical trajectory, to use the terminology of systems thinking' (p. 25). The development of ideas, he claims, will be different in each context; each history will have its own cognitive phylogeny. For Renfrew, 'mind' is the formulated concepts and the shared ways of thought which, within any specific cultural matrix, are the common inheritance of all its citizens as participants (p. 26).

There is an internal contradiction within this natural science-derived *and* historically relative point of view. On the one hand 'we' in the present and 'they' in the past have our own cultural matrices, our different ways of thought within which 'we' and 'they' perceive(d) the world of things and objects. On the other hand there is postulated a universal method and coherent theory which relates ways of thought to material objects. How can my coherent theory and explicit methodology about the relationship between the material and the ideal be applied to another culture with its own cognitive processes and 'cognitive phylogeny'?

There is no problem of inference within the systemic

approach as long as one remains fully materialist. As long as one says, 'I can predict ideas, thought and cognition from the economic base using a covering law, and the economic base can be objectively perceived and measured', there is no difficulty. But as soon as one says this, the lack of humanism is apparent; and in discussing 'mind' Flannery and Marcus and Renfrew have adopted a normative and partially idealist position within which cognition and perception are not universally determined by the material base, but are partly historically contingent, based on particular cultural phylogenies. As soon as one admits some cultural relativity in this way an insuperable contradiction emerges. It is no longer possible to have a universal natural science theory and method which will allow secure inference and prediction from one historical context to another.

It will be necessary, then, in the quest for an adequate archaeology of mind, to ditch decisively the natural science, covering law approach. Following Collingwood, we shall see that the inferential procedures followed routinely by archaeologists include reconstructing past cultural matrices 'from the inside'. The implications of the collapse of the natural science model in confrontation with mind will be shown later in this book to be far-reaching.

Conclusion

In this chapter I have equated systems theory in archaeology with Gellner's covering law approach. A relationship between systems analysis and law-and-order models has been specifically denied by Flannery (1973), who argues that the analysis of processual inter-relationships does not necessitate the imposition of covering laws.

There is certainly a sense in which systems thinking is contextual. The aim is to examine the way in which a particular set of components are related into a whole. It might be thought that the method, or way of thinking, does not involve any universal laws; however, as with all methodologies, this one is

theory-bound. It certainly is difficult to represent other viewpoints, such as Marxist notions of contradiction, conflict and
dialectic, within a systems framework. Equally, the method
does not allow for a structuralist conception of society of the
form culture:nature::male:female.

The very method does assume some specific general principles. In particular it assumes that societies can be divided
into sub-systems – separate types of activity. For example, I
would find it difficult to decide whether a 'meal' today was in
the economic, social or ritual sub-system, or which parts of
the 'meal' should be in which sub-system. I would certainly be
highly suspicious if it was claimed that 'meals' were in the
same sub-system in all societies. In addition it is assumed that
explanation of one type of activity (such as ritual) always involves reference to something outside itself (another sub-
system such as the social sphere). We explain one thing by its
functions in relation to something else. I would again find this
unsatisfactory in relation to an English 'meal'. While the utilitarian, social and ideological functions are part of the explanation of the 'meal', it seems to me that the meal must partly be
understood as being organized in ways that are not reducible
to external functions.

While the notion of functionally related sub-systems is a
clear cross-cultural theory, it is not necessarily the case that
systems theory is materialist: there is no necessity for the
material base to be primary. However, in practice, as we have
seen, it does tend to have a dominant role in relation to which
society and ideology function. This underlying viewpoint is
identical to Hawkes' (1954) ladder of inference. An important
aspect of systems theory in archaeology is that it has allowed
movement up this ladder in a systematic fashion. For Hawkes,
the technology, and to a lesser extent the economy of past systems were attainable, but higher up the ladder, social organization and religion were largely beyond reach. Daniel (1962,
pp. 134–5) accepted that artifacts are the product of the human
mind but said that there is no coincidence between the
material and non-material aspects of culture. Systems theory
provides a method for bringing the social (Renfrew 1973) and

the ideational (Renfrew 1983a) into the domain of feasible study, because systematic links between the material world and these less visible aspects of life could be predicted. For example, links have been demonstrated between subsistence categories and burial practices (Binford 1971), between stress and 'generalized feather-waving' (Johnson 1982, p. 405), and between increased production and increased ritual (Drennan 1976, p. 360).

Systems theory may have bridged the credibility gap in relation to archaeological study of the ideational realm, but in this chapter I have tried to show that it has not taken us very much farther along the road. The approach is not able to account for the great richness, variability and specificity of cultural production, and individuals and their shared thoughts are passive by-products of 'the system'. Human activity is timeless, the product of systemic inter-relationships rather than being historically derived. Above all, the approach in archaeology has led to an internally self-contradictory epistemology. No wonder alternative approaches are now being sought.

Underlying all the criticisms that have been made of systems analysis in this chapter is the implication that such analysis occurs only at a 'surface' level. The procedures involve measuring directly sizes of settlements, numbers of figurines, population infill and expansion and so on. All these 'observable' data are then inter-related, and in computer simulation a set of mathematical equations may be applied. Abstract theories (such as the primacy of the material base) are of course accommodated to the data, but the impression that is gained is that all is as it seems to be. If the term 'structure' is used at all in such analyses it is equivalent to the term 'system'.

But throughout this chapter there have been intimations of another level of analysis. Why is the system or sub-system the way it is, why the sting-ray spine, why burials and not hoards to display social rivalry, why feather-waving and not pot-smashing, and what structures the 'meal'? There is perhaps an order or structure behind these cultural choices that systems theory is not allowing us to approach.

And we have begun to see the importance of interpreting

symbolic meanings rather than just ascribing symbolic functions. For example, we cannot discuss the social functions of
tombs without also discussing what they meant. We need,
then, to turn to an approach which looks at structure and at
the meaning of signs.

3 Structuralist archaeology

When Edmund Leach (1973) suggested that archaeology would soon turn from functionalism to structuralism, following the path of social anthropology, he was clearly unaware that structuralist archaeology already existed. In particular the work of Leroi-Gourhan (1965), similar in some respects to that of Levi-Strauss, had been widely debated. Certainly structuralism has never dominated the discipline, but its widespread attraction cannot be denied (Bintliff 1984; Deetz 1983; Huffman 1981; 1984; Kent 1984; Leone 1978; Miller 1982a; Muller 1971; Richards and Thomas 1984; Schnapp 1984; Van de Velde 1980). These various articles, in addition to those to be discussed in this chapter, suggest that one can now talk of a structuralist archaeology.

Yet why has the analysis of 'structured sets of differences' been so slow to arrive and so slight in impact? Why has structuralism never formed a major coherent alternative in archaeology? The first answer to these questions is that structuralism is not a coherent approach itself, since it covers a great variety of work, from the structural linguistics of Saussure, and the generative grammar of Chomsky, to the developmental psychology of Piaget and the analysis of 'deep' meanings by Levi-Strauss. In archaeology this variety is reflected in the differences between the formal analyses of Washburn (1983) and Hillier *et al* (1976), the Piagetian accounts of Wynn (1979; and see Paddaya 1981), and the Levi-Strauss type of analyses conducted by Leroi-Gourhan (1965; 1982).

The second answer is that, linked to this variability, some structuralist approaches in archaeology could fit within processual archaeology, almost unnoticed, and working towards the same ends as New Archaeology. Fritz (1978), for example, discusses the adaptive value of spatial and symbolic codes. Indeed there are many close similarities between systems analysis and structuralism, and we shall see below that the criticisms of both run parallel. The most obvious similarity between the two methods is that both are concerned with 'systemness'. The emphasis is on inter-relationships between entities: the aim of both systems and structuralist analysis is to provide some organization which will allow us to fit all the parts into a coherent whole. In systems analysis this structure is a flow diagram, sometimes with mathematical functions describing the relationships between the sub-systems; the system is more than, or larger than, the component parts, but it exists at the same level of analysis. Although in structuralism the structures exist at a deeper level, the parts are again linked to a whole by binary oppositions, generative rules and so on. In both systems and structuralist analysis it is the relationship between parts that is most important.

A further similarity between systems theory and structuralism is that both sometimes claim to involve rigorous analysis of observable data. In some types of structuralist archaeology (particularly that which I shall describe as formal analysis) the structures and conceptual schemes are thought to be empirical and measurable. In systems theory there is a close link to positivism, in that by measuring covariation between variables observable in the real world, the system can be identified and verified. While positivism is an 'ideology' expressed by some structural and formal analysts in archaeology, we shall see that, as in systems analysis, the apparent 'hardness' of the data and rigour of the method are illusory.

A third answer to the question of why structuralism never offered a coherent set of alternatives in archaeology, lies in the fact that while some types of structuralism (such as formal analysis) were *perceived* to be rigorous and 'hard', other types (particularly work modelled on that carried out by Levi-Strauss) were *perceived* to be 'soft' and unscientific. In particular, it was thought that it would be impossible to verify hypotheses about structures of meaning, especially since much structuralist analysis outside archaeology has concerned myths. Archaeology, with its dominant perception of itself as positivist and materialist, could scarcely launch itself with any confidence into such an arena. As Wylie (1982) has shown, all types of archaeology involve moving beyond the data in order to interpret them, and structuralism is no different in this respect. Yet the dominant archaeological perspective of science was antithetical to structuralism.

Given these three reasons for a sceptical reaction in archaeology to Leach's claims, the type of structuralism that could most easily be placed within processual archaeology, and which will be discussed first here, was formal analysis, which purports to describe the real world rather than to divine inner essences.

Formal analysis and generative grammars

With the structural linguistics of Saussure, the sign itself is seen as arbitrary and conventional. In other words any symbol (a bead, duck, arrowhead) *could* be used to signify a chief; there is no necessary relationship between the signifier (the bead) and the signified (chiefness). Because of this arbitrariness, Saussure's analysis of meaning concentrates on structured sets of differences. Thus the bead, indicating 'chiefness', is contrasted with the lack of bead, or presence of another item, signifying 'non-chiefness'. Analysis is of *form* not content.

Formal analyses in archaeology are best exemplified by the work of Washburn (1983), who has concentrated on the way symmetry rules can be identified and compared within and between cultures. Examination of pottery designs, for example, can produce classifications not based on design motifs, but on the way the motifs are organized in symmetrical relationships. The main types of symmetry recognized are shown in Fig. 2. The concern is not, then, with whether a comma, triangle or star are used as the design motif, since ethnographic research (cf. Hardin 1970) has shown that design content is not a good indicator of group affiliation. Design structure is thought to be a more stable measure of cultural groupings.

Symmetry analysis is in many respects non-generative. It is concerned with examining pattern as it exists, static, on a pot surface, and identifying underlying structure. On the other hand symmetry can be described as a rule which generates pat-

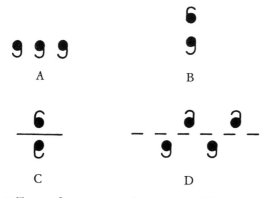

Fig. 2. Types of symmetry and repetition of design. (A) Translation. (B) Bifold rotation. (C) Horizontal mirror reflection. (D) Slide reflection. Source: Washburn 1983

terns. Chomsky emphasized 'rule-governed creativity', and, in an analysis of calabash decoration amongst the Nuba of Sudan, a generative grammar was claimed (Hodder 1982a), following the analyses published by Faris (1972).

To talk of a design grammar or language is to note the origins of structuralist analysis in Saussure's structural linguistics. In the Nuba case the grammar was derived from a cross motif (Fig. 3:1). Both 'words' and 'grammatical rules' were suggested and shown to be able to produce a wide variety of calabash decoration, from highly organized designs (Fig. 3:10) to apparently 'random' designs. Thus, the band of bow-tie motifs in Fig. 3:15 can be produced by taking the triangle 'word', and attaching another at the angle (not at the side): ▶◀ . This 'bow-tie' motif is then, according to another rule, rotated through units of 90° to produce ▶◀▶◀ etc. In all the calabash designs depicted in Fig. 3, the rules are kept to: the 'words' join at the angles (not at the sides) and so on.

Washburn (1983, p. 138) claims that symmetry analysis allows systematic and objective measurement and comparison of designs through time and across broad areas. Formal analyses of settlement structure (cf. Hillier *et al* 1976; Fletcher 1977) appear to offer a similar promise. In all these cases it appears that we can describe structures and test them rigorously against

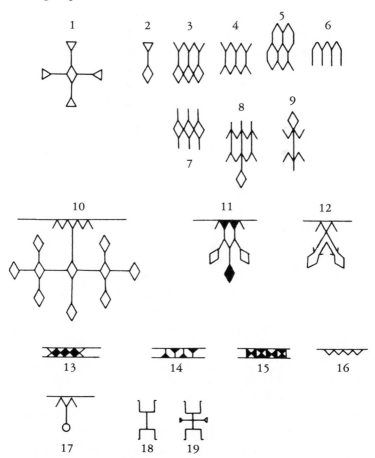

Fig. 3. Nuba designs using a grammar derived from a cross motif (1). The 'words' of the grammar are the triangle, line and diamond in the cross, and the 'rules' include joining words at angles rather than sides, and rotation in units of 90°. Source: Hodder 1982a.

the data. Statistical tests can be carried out (Fletcher 1977) and the grammars simulated on a computer (Hodder 1982a) to see whether they really do generate the observed patterns. Such work then, appears not to involve risky leaps of faith: apparently no meaning is assigned and there is much scientific rigour. The analysis is purely formal. As a result such work can easily be placed within positivist New Archaeology – it offers no threat, particularly when linked to systems interpretations (see below).

Is it really the case, however, that formal analyses do not involve the imposition of meaning, that they are not concerned with content? Let us take as an example Washburn's analysis of the chevron design $\lll\lll$. Her concern is to eliminate 'subjective design labels' such as 'chevron' (1983, p. 143), and she prefers instead 'Class 1–110: one dimensional designs generated by horizontal mirror reflection'. Washburn suggests that the chevron design has been generated by placing an horizontal axis through the 'chevrons' and seeing the upper part as a mirror reflection of the bottom part:

$$\lll\lll = - \frac{\text{\large 6}}{\text{\large e}} - = \text{horizontal mirror reflection}$$

An alternative analysis would be to take the units of design not as the individual slanting designs but as the chevron:

$$\lll\lll = \text{\bf 9 9 9 9} \quad = \text{translation}$$

Washburn attempts to avoid such ambiguities by defining the unit of analysis precisely as the smallest asymmetrical element (such as the comma). However, clearly lines and circles cannot be fitted into such a scheme, and the definition is itself arbitrary: while it may assist objective analysis, it may hide other levels of symmetrical relationships as in the chevron example above. Equally, the axis along which symmetry is sought is an interpretation, not a description, of the data. Put another way, the symmetrical analysis is a description within a set of interpretive decisions. Thus, such analyses *do* involve giving meaning to content – they are not just formal descriptions to aid comparison. To perceive a mark on a pot as 'a unit of analysis', or as a 'design motif', is to give meaning to that mark, to interpret its content, and, whether we like it or not, it involves trying to see the design as prehistoric people saw it.

I shall return to this latter point later in this volume, but for the moment it is important to recognize that the subjectivity lying behind Washburn's supposed objectivity in no way detracts from her work. Rather such subjectivity is a necessary component of all archaeological analysis. We have seen the pervasiveness of the problems of perception in post-positivist philosophy (pp. 14 to 16). All archaeological analyses are based on subjective categories (pot types, settlement sites, etc) and unobservable structural or systemic relationships (positive and negative feedback, exchange relationships and so on). In the imposition of Thiessen polygons on a settlement pattern, for example, we can never be sure that our 'units of analysis' (the sites or nodes in the settlement pattern) are really comparable. We have to give them meaning (as settlement sites, towns, cities) before we can suggest systemic and structural relationships between or behind them.

The 'hard' nature of formal analysis is thus illusory. That symmetry analysis, for example, can be slotted into archaeology without threat is because the whole of archaeology is guided by the same ideology of positivism, as a result of which there has been very little attempt to push beyond the symmetries in pottery decoration to the content of the message(s). The interpretation of symbolic meaning has been minimized in favour of direct links between symmetry and processes of social interaction. For example, Washburn suggests that 'identity in design structure seems to be indicative of homogeneous cultural composition and intensity of cultural interaction' (1983, p. 140). This may well be a fruitful hypothesis, 'tested' within ethnographic interpretations and successfully applied to archaeological data (*ibid.*), but by linking design form to society in this direct way we overlook the very real possibility that design structure may have different meanings in different cultural contexts. To what extent can we assume that subjectively defined design structures will have universal social implications? A properly rigorous and hence scientific analysis needs also to examine the symbolic meanings which mediate between structure (of design) and social functions.

Structuralist analysis

When we ask for the meaning of the symmetries or other formal structures, when we consider whether the symmetries in
the pottery decoration are transformations of those in the
organization of settlement space, or in burial practices, and
when we relate such structures to abstract structures in the
mind, we begin to move from formal to structuralist analysis.

It could be argued that the assignment of concepts to parts
or wholes of structures, as in the work of Leroi-Gourhan (1965;
1982), differs not at all from the assignment of meaning to
marks scratched on pots when defining design motifs. Perhaps
the only difference is that the assignment of meaning in the
latter type of work, as exemplified by Washburn's careful and
persuasive analyses, is masked within objective science. The
earlier work of Leroi-Gourhan, on the other hand, involved a
self-conscious attempt to assign meaning. At the same time,
the Leroi-Gourhan type of work is potentially more 'scientific'
in the sense that it does involve bringing one's 'meanings' out
into the open rather than applying them covertly.

Too often, however, structures have been identified and
compared in archaeology without an adequate consideration
of meaning content – this criticism can be levelled, for example, at work on Dutch Neolithic pottery (Hodder 1982b).
Here a transformation of structures was identified, from
'bounded' designs in which a hierarchy of horizontal/vertical
oppositions could be identified, to horizontally zoned, 'additive' sequences (Fig. 4). The earlier bounded designs were
linked directly to bounded social entities (lineage groups),
while the later additive designs expressed the incorporation of
groups within extensive social networks. Such interpretation
remains implausible because there is no reason for us to expect
any relationship between pot decoration and these aspects of
social organization. Before we can interpret the social functions of the decoration we need to obtain some idea of what
the designs and the pots mean. We need to consider whether
the pots are domestic, ritual, prestige, whether the decoration
varies between pots with different uses, whether the decor-

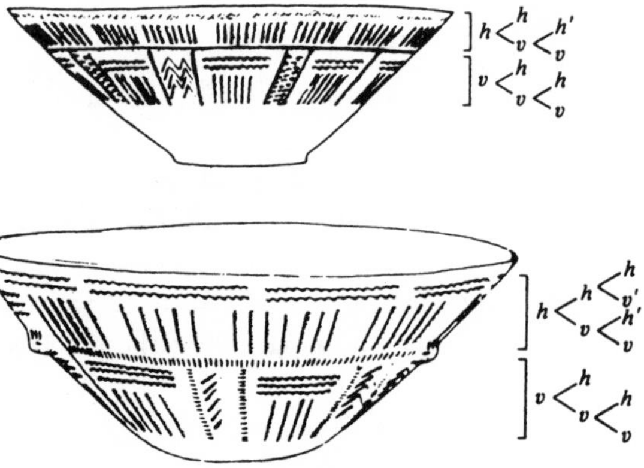

Fig. 4. Change in design structure in the Dutch Neolithic. (A) Dendritic structure built up from horizontal and vertical contrasts on TRB pottery; h′ or v′ indicates a horizontal/vertical contrast produced by the use of a blank area. (B) Sequential structure built up from alternating zones on PFB pottery; A′ indicates a transformation of the A design. Source: Hodder 1982b.

ation exists on other artifacts, what are the contexts of decoration in this culture generally, and so on. As we get closer to these contextual meanings it is easier to link the design structures to the social functions they fulfilled.

A further example clarifies the point. Arnold (1983) shows how basic principles of organizing and utilizing environmental and social space in Quinua, Peru, are reflected in the organization of decorative space on painted vessels. The environmental space around the potting community is organized into a series of horizontally bedded ecological zones from lowland to upland, all of which need to be exploited to allow community self-sufficiency. Arnold relates the horizontal zoning in the environment to the horizontally zoned decoration on the pots; in addition, those environmental zones with fixed unvarying exploitation are reflected in the relative lack of variability in motifs on the equivalent zones on the pots. A cross-cutting division of the environment and society into two communities linked to a divided irrigation system is equated

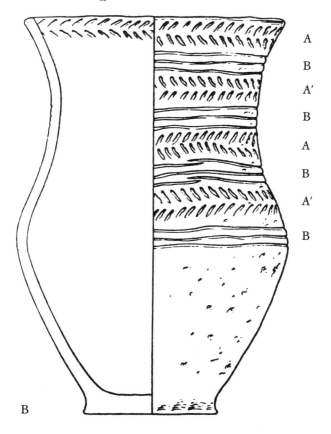

A
B
A'
B
A
B
A'
B

by Arnold with the use of bilateral symmetry in the pottery decoration.

Arnold provides very little contextual information which would support the hypothesized links between design structure and environment. The problem is: why should anyone believe that there is a relationship between the two types of zoning? Is this not an example of the analyst playing with patterns and always finding something that fits? Before the interpretations can be believable, the abstract structures (horizontal zones, bilateral symmetry) have to be grounded in the context of use and the content of meaning in specific cultural situations. Arnold briefly mentions that the pots analysed are utility water vessels which have a common function with the spatial organization of the community based on water distribution. The plausibility of the account would be increased by exploring further such linkages and associations. Is there any pictorial representation suggesting that pots, zones, motifs do 'mean' environmental zones, up/down and so on?

In the above examples the design structure is related to other structures without adequate consideration of the context of use of the artifacts involved, or of their meaning content. Much the same can be said of several structural analyses of settlement patterns. For example, Fritz (1978) identifies symmetrical relationships in the organization of settlement in Chaco Canyon. The balanced and unbalanced symmetries (arranged W–E, N–S) occur at both regional and within-settlement scales. The structural arrangements are then said to be adaptive, relating to hierarchical social structure on the one hand and symmetrical social relationships on the other. While there is some concern to give cultural meanings (e.g. sacred/ profane) to the spatial oppositions, the plausibility of the argument would be increased if more attention were paid to the content of the settlement space in the Chaco Canyon context. What do north or the N–S axis mean at the different scales? We must await more evidence about what the various sites and parts of sites in the settlement pattern were used for.

Without some notion of the meaning content of decorative or spatial elements, it is difficult to see how the structures of signification can be interpreted in relation to other aspects of life. But how are the meanings to be assigned? Here we can return to the pioneering work of Leroi-Gourhan. He certainly assigned meaning (male, female) to the paintings on Palaeolithic cave walls, and the validity of his work has been discussed from many angles. In my view, the inadequacies of his work derive not from the attempt to interpret meaning, since, as we have seen, the assignment of meaning to material culture is a necessary stage of analysis. Rather, the inadequacies derive from our limited information as to the Palaeolithic and from an unwillingness to criticize the universality of our own assumptions. Leroi-Gourhan has little information available to him regarding the signs used in the parietal art. There is a limited degree to which the designs can be followed through into other cultural domains (burial, artifacts, settlement space) in order to indentify their associations. One cannot easily identify the particular meanings of these design motifs in the South-West French Palaeolithic context, simply because the data are limited.

To interpret meaning contents one has to be willing to make abstractions from associations and contrasts in the archaeological record. This can be done with greater care and rigour where – unlike the Upper Palaeolithic – there is more associational information in different types of data. An example of associational, contextual analysis, in which meanings are assigned and links are made between structures occurring in different activities, is provided by McGhee's (1977) consideration of prehistoric archaeological remains from the Thule culture of arctic Canada. The initial observation was that ivory and sea mammal bone are associated with harpoon heads, while arrowheads are made of antler. In trying to understand this dichotomy, McGhee looked at the other associations of ivory and antler in Thule culture. Ivory was used for items associated with sea mammal hunting: snow goggles, kayak mountings, dog trace buckles and so on. Other items made from ivory are those connected with women and with winter activities: needle cases, thimble holders, female ornaments, small bird–woman figures. Antler, on the other hand, is linked to land mammals, particularly the caribou, men and summer life on land. The following structure thus emerges, based on the contextual associations of antler and ivory:

land:sea::summer:winter::man:woman::antler:ivory

This structured set of differences is supported further by showing that there is no functional reason why antler and ivory need to be used for different hunting tools and weapons. In addition, ethnographic and historic evidence indicates that the Inuit concept of their environment was centred around the dichotomy between land and sea. The meat of caribou and sea mammals could not be cooked in the same pot. Caribou skins could not be sewn on the sea ice. Associations between women and sea mammals and between land, men and summer life are also found in historic Inuit mythology. Such evidence is not of a radically different nature to the archaeological data; it simply supplies more contextual information concerning the hypothesized structure and its meaning.

McGhee's analysis provides a clear example of the way in which structuralist analysis has the potential for rigour, when combined with an analysis of context and content (i.e. that ivory is associated with sea mammals and women in the Thule culture). It seems reasonable to expect that, as the 'hard' nature of archaeological science becomes demystified, some types of structuralist analysis involving the assigning of meaning will become more common and acceptable. There is an enormous potential, scarcely tapped at the moment, for careful analysis. For example, it is possible to identify differences in the use of left/right, front/back, centre/periphery parts of houses, settlements, cemeteries, graves, ritual sites and so on. Other dichotomies between ritual and mundane, life and death can also be sought. All such structuralist analysis includes some imposition of meaning content.

A further example of potential interest is domestic/wild in relation to inside/outside settlement. Here one can examine the degree of elaboration within the two spheres. For example, in the earlier parts of the European Neolithic it is the domestic context which is elaborated – domestic pottery is highly decorated, houses are substantial and complex. Moving through the Neolithic, domestic elaboration decreases so that domestic pottery becomes undecorated, and houses insubstantial, while elaboration occurs in the 'wild', as seen in deliberate ritual hoarding in wet areas, elaborate burial away from settlements, or the growth of rock art depicting outdoor, male activities such as animal herding but not depicting domestic activities. It is also possible that the percentage of wild animals on sites increases at the moment when 'defensive' boundaries around settlements disappear. Such changing emphases on the domestic and wild, culture and nature, have yet to be examined in any detail in archaeology (see, however, Richards and Thomas 1984). The boundary around a settlement has yet to be discussed as a symbolic division in relation to the types of data just described (but see Hall 1976). The archaeological consideration of certain types of analysis remains caught within its own masking ideology.

Critique

Although the concern of this book is to seek an adequate account of the relationship between the material and ideal, the contribution of Levi-Strauss is primarily towards a theory of the superstructure. The relationships with the infrastructure are not the prime focus of study.

Following the semiotic approach to linguistics in the work of Saussure, which had a major influence on structuralism, the concern is to examine the organization of signs so that they have meaning. Thus, the word 'pot' is an arbitrary *signifier* of the concept *signified*.

'pot'

signifier   *signified*   *object*

One studies the relationship between signifier and signified, but there is little interest in the 'thing' itself – in this case the real material pot. Such approaches do not help us in our search for the relationships between ideal and material.

The abstract analysis of signs and meanings is particularly a problem in archaeology, which is primarily concerned with material culture. We dig up material as much as we dig up ideas. And we wish to see each object *both* as an object, the result of processes of production and action, *and* as a sign, since the object (pot) can itself be the signifier for other concepts (such as tribe 'x', or female activities). The study of material culture invites us to bridge the gap between ideal and material, but structuralism gives us little assistance in this domain.

In seeking for the relationships between structure and process (that is the recursiveness of structure and action), structuralism plays a necessary but insufficient role. The word 'pot' can be the signifier for the concept of a pot. But, equally, the object itself can be the signifier for the idea of what is a pot – there are influences both ways. Structures permit, are the media for, action in the world, but they are also changed by those actions.

The same critical comment can be made in a somewhat different way. Once again, in structuralism, the individual is passive. Rather than being determined by adaptive regulatory laws, the individual is now determined by structures and/or universals of the human mind. The inadequacy of this view can be seen by asking the question 'what is good style?' in relation to design or any structured domain of activity. To be 'stylish' is not simply a matter of doggedly following the rules. O'Neale (1932) found that North Coast Californian Indian basket weavers said that designs were 'good' if they were pleasing and well arranged, while badly structured designs were thought 'bad'. But such verbal evidence simply supports the notion that a structured style exists – within the structure, or even transgressing it, it is still possible to be 'stylish'. A 'pop star', such as Boy George, can create a new style and be thought highly stylish even though no design grammar could ever have generated his selection of clothes, ornaments and sexual innuendos. Rather, Boy George creates style by using, playing on and transforming structural rules concerning clothing. He uses structure socially to create new structure and new society.

Thus our theories about structure must allow the role of the active individual. In much structuralist archaeology the rules appear to make up a set of shared norms: everyone in society is assumed to have the same structures, to see them from the same angle and to give them the same meaning. This is a strongly normative view which (as was outlined in chapter 1) this book seeks to question.

The final aspect of the critique, closely related to the rest, is that structuralism is ahistorical in two senses. First, Saussure emphasized the arbitrariness of the sign. Any word could have been used to signify the concept of a pot, and any object or space could have been used to signify boundedness, sexuality, tribal group, summer and winter. Such an approach is clearly lacking in a discipline which can follow the way in which signs come to have non-arbitrary meanings through long-term historical sequences. Second, it is unclear how structural changes occur. Certainly one can always say that change involves structural transformation and this notion is an important one; but within the structuralist analyses themselves there is little need for change, and it is difficult to see why the transformations occur, why they do so in a certain direction, and why or how the structures themselves might change radically. This problem again results from the inadequate linkage between structure and process and from the minimal role given to the active individual in the creation of structures.

Verification

Perhaps the major critique of structuralism centres around the notion of verification. How does one do structuralist archaeology with rigour? Structuralism is notoriously linked to unverifiable flights of fancy, ungrounded arguments, since all the data can, with imagination, be seen as transformations of each other and of underlying structures. Many structuralist analyses *do* appear rigorous and have been widely accepted. The perception that one can judge structuralist analyses and decide that some are better than others, implies that procedures for making plausible arguments can be discerned (Wylie 1982).

The most widespread validation procedure adopted in structuralist archaeology appears to be to demonstrate that the same structures lie behind many different types of data in the same historical context. The more data that can be slotted into the same organizing principles, the more plausibility is gained by the organizing principles themselves. As with systems analysis, structuralist analysis is convincing if it can draw together, or make sense of, previously unconnected disparate data. As we have seen, simply looking for pattern (horizontal and vertical zoning, symmetry and so on) is inadequate – we also need to make some abstraction about the meaning of the pattern. Thus, in Deetz's (1977) convincing analysis of refuse discard, burial, and pottery styles on historic American sites, a temporal contrast between abstractions which he calls communal and individualizing ethics can be seen to run through the study, and to explain a wide variety of different types of data.

David Clarke (1972) in his study of structural relationships in the Iron Age, Glastonbury site, supported his case by showing the repetition of the same male:female structure in different living compounds and in different time periods. Fritz (1978) sought to find the same structure at local and regional levels. Tilley (1984) shows how an abstraction termed 'boundedness' can be observed to change at the same time in both pottery decoration and burial ritual. In an analysis of the Orkney Neolithic, I attempted to show that structures in settlement, burial and ritual uses of space could be correlated, although the data were scarcely adequate (Hodder 1982a).

The question of verification of structure – does the structure relate to the data? – is a conventional one. All archaeological analysis involves interpreting the real world in the process of observation, and then fitting one's theories to these observations in order to make a plausible, accommodative argument – claims to do anything else are illusory. Structuralist analysis proceeds by the same principles. For example, in the analysis of the Nuba art (see above, p. 37), the more art, and the more varied the art, that the generative grammar can generate, the more plausible is the grammar. We can ask whether any designs occur which do not fit the rules. For example, are the 'words' ever joined at the sides rather than at the angles? In fact —▶ rarely, if ever, occurs in the art. The same applies to ❥ . These motifs are not allowed by the grammar, and that they do not occur in the art supports the grammar itself.

It is important to recognize that the structures need not be universal, and their proposed universality should not be a major part of the validation procedure. The structures them-selves may be quite specific (as in the Nuba use of the cross design). But it is the meaning content especially that may have particular historical significance. Thus the Nuba cross is not just a design structure – it is a highly emotive symbol, with a strong but particular historical significance which affects its social use in Nuba art (Hodder 1982a). Part of the validation of structuralist analyses in archaeology must therefore con-cern the abstraction of particular meanings related to the structures.

In some cases, where there is historical continuity with the present, meanings assigned to the past appear convincing. Thus, Glassie's (1975) identification of certain types of build-ing, facades, room spaces, as 'public' or 'private', or his associ-ation of asymmetry with 'nature' and 'the organic', is convincing because eighteenth-century America is close to us. I would personally be much less convinced if asymmetry were related to 'the organic' in Kenya or in prehistoric Hungary. It is when meanings are applied cross-culturally, without reference to context, that the dangers emerge. Thus, in his recent work, Leroi-Gourhan (1982) is much more cautious about identify-ing 'male' or 'female' designs in Palaeolithic caves. But in pre-historic periods where more contextual and associational data are present, the imputation of meaning can be carefully con-structed. Thus, in the Neolithic of Europe, I have argued that the tombs mean houses on the basis of eight points of similarity between them (Hodder 1984a). Contextual and functional associations also allow a commonality of meaning to be in-ferred. Clearly we cannot assume with confidence that if an object is found in a male grave it has 'male' qualities, or that an artifact found in a ceremonial site has 'ritual' meanings, but such assumptions are routinely made by archaeologists. By careful and critical consideration of context, the meanings can be made plausible. For example, Arnold suggests that the zon-ing of the environment and the zoned decoration on the pots are associated in this particular cultural context, because both the pots and the zoned environment have common water management functions. By making such contextual links

Arnold increases the plausibility of his argument, which would be further strengthened if it could be shown that the water pots were the only ones used in the horizontally zoned environment, or that pots used for other purposes were not decorated in the same way.

It might be thought that a dichotomy ought to be presented between structural and functional explanation, suggesting that an important way of supporting a theory about the one is to show that the data are not adequately explained by the other. Certainly, McGhee supports his case by suggesting that there is no functional need for ivory and antler to be used for different categories of tool and weapon. This type of argument is dangerous in that it often assumes a primacy of the material, functional side: the functions are explained first, and anything left over is 'mind'. But the argument also fallaciously assumes that there is a dichotomy between function and symbolic meaning. As McGhee's example shows, an item may be part of a tool-kit, but at the same time it may be part of a structured set of categories. As archaeologists, we may take depositional and post-depositional factors into account and still find functional associations between objects on our sites. Such functional linkages play a part in the meanings assigned to objects – part of the symbolic and cognitive significance of objects derives from their use. In chapter 2 we saw that the assignment of function depends on imputing symbolic meaning. Once again we return here to the notions of material culture as both object and sign, of two-way influences, of a necessary unity.

A purely hypothetical example may clarify the point. Imagine that some prehistoric long houses have been found in a region. They are all aligned NW–SE, with the entrances at the SE ends. Two 'conflicting' hypotheses are suggested: either the alignment is because the prevailing wind is from the NW, or the NW–SE axis has symbolic significance. Both hypotheses can be supported in their varying ways, the one by showing that the prevailing wind was indeed from the NW, the other by identifying the same structure in other domains. For example, the same NW–SE axis might be found in burial and ritual sites, and in other aspects of the use of space in settlements. But in fact the two hypotheses are not contradictory. In giving meaning to the world around us we commonly make use of the positions of the sun, moon, rivers, hills, and wind; equally, the symbolic significance attached to wind and its prevailing axis will affect decisions about how to arrange houses and settlements. Thus functional use and environmental features are parts of the process of giving meaning to the world, and validation of meaning structures should not depend on ironing out such factors.

We have seen that plausible structuralist arguments can be made by showing that the structures account for much, and many different categories of, data. It is also necessary to ground the structures in their meaning content and in their context of use. In these various ways one can show, in the data, that certain arguments just do not hold water. Thus an item that is supposed to be 'male' is found in a female grave, or a phase of 'communal' activities has many 'individualing' characteristics, or too many arrowheads are made of ivory. Of course one could argue that a 'transformation' of the structure has occurred in the cases that do not 'fit', but at some stage one's intellectual ingenuity becomes implausible, at least to others, and different structures are sought to account for the data.

Conclusion: the importance of structuralist archaeology

In this chapter the emphasis has moved to symbolic codes and structures of the mind. In the next chapter other types of structure, technological and social, will be described. The major importance of all such work in archaeology is that it takes us to another level of analysis. We are no longer bound to the quantification of presences, but we are also drawn to the interpretation of absences. The system is no longer all that there is – there are also structures through which it takes its form. We still have not adequately found the individual in a cultural and historical context, as the critique above makes clear, but we have come some way along our road, particularly in the understanding of culture as meaningfully constituted.

Structuralism provides a method and a theory for the analysis of material culture meanings. Processual archaeologists have been largely concerned with the functions of symbols. As we have seen, function is an important aspect of meaning: the use and association of a pot with its contents, with the fire on which the pot's contents are cooked, with tribal identity and with the social hierarchy, are all important in, although not determinant of, the pot's symbolic meanings. But processual archaeologists have not been concerned with the organization of these functional associations into meaning structures. Whatever the limitations of structuralism, it provides a first step towards a broader approach.

Moreover, structuralism, in whatever guise, contributes to archaeology, of whatever character, the notion of transformation. Schiffer (1976), of course, has noted the importance of cultural transforms, but structuralism supplies a method and a deeper level of analysis. As Faris (1983) points out, material culture does not represent social relations – rather it represents a subjective way of viewing social relations. From work on artifact discard showing that notions of 'dirt' intervene between residues and societies (Okely 1979; Moore 1982), to work showing that burial is a conceptual transformation of society (Parker Pearson 1982), the structuralist contribution is clear. The rules of transformation can be approached, it is claimed, through systematic analysis.

A related and equally important contribution is that different spheres of material culture and of human activity (burial, settlement, art, exchange) may be transformations of the same underlying schemes, or may be transformations of each other. Rather than seeing each domain as a separate sub-system, each can be related to the other as different outward manifestations of the same code. The importance of the notion that culture is meaningfully constituted is clear in this drawing together of the various strands of archaeological data and analysis.

4 Marxist archaeology, ideology and practice

If archaeologists are to incorporate the notion of structure into their processual studies, it must be recognized that the structures may be of many different types and occur at many different levels. There are other structures beside those of the mind: in this chapter, approaches will be discussed which examine structures in technology, economy and particularly in social processes.

It is not difficult to see that many different technological processes, and the nature of their varied products, may be influenced by some common underlying themes, ranging from the form of operational sequences to the type of gestures and hand movements involved. Whether cereal grains are pounded with a vertical motion or ground with a horizontal motion may be linked to the way clay is broken up (by vertical or horizontal movements) prior to potting. Perhaps the major attempt to classify such differences in a wide range of technical processes has been made by Leroi-Gourhan (1943; 1945), and there is renewed interest in examining structures and operational chains in the area of techniques (Cresswell 1972; Lemonnier 1976; Digard 1979). Given an initial series of choices and constraints there is a necessary underlying logic to many technical processes. An example is provided by Tolstoy's (1966, p. 72) account of what he terms a 'logical structure' in bark cloth making:

> Removing the bast layer is an obligatory task. It involves an obligatory decision on the part of the manufacturer, and may be performed in one of four alternative ways. Boiling the bast, on the other hand, is optional. Some kind of beater is necessary, but only the selection of a 2-piece design raises the contingent problem of attaching the head to the handle, to which there are four known major solutions.

The logical relationships between interlocking decisions within technological processes can be discussed as independent technological structures, but it is also possible to examine the social structures which play a role in technological systems – and here a full discussion has been provided by Lemonnier (1983; 1984), including consideration of the technical act as sign.

The main concern in this volume is with idea and meaning, and, unfortunately, the links that have been made between the technological and the ideational often appear over-simplistic. Childe (1949, p. 22) suggested that the appearance of rotary mills in Athenian bakeries allowed causality to be depersonalized, but with the appearance in Europe of machines operated by the impersonal forces of water, wind, steam and electricity, causality became completely mechanistic. Haudricourt (1962) connected the Mediterranean type of cereal agriculture and herding, characterized by 'direct positive action' on the food resources, with a view of humanity in the West where leaders are seen as shepherds, pastors. In the East, however, 'indirect negative action' on resources leads to a different view of humanity, seen especially in China and in Confucianism, where good government emanates from the virtue of its subjects.

While such studies remain abstract and difficult to evaluate, it is nevertheless possible that the organization of technical processes may be linked in important ways to structures of meaning. Miller (1982b) has shown how the elaboration of pottery production methods in contemporary India must be understood within a particular set of attitudes, concerning, for example, the caste system. As another example, given the need to produce a cutting edge from flint, many procedures can be followed, some more complex, multi-staged and formal, others more immediate and simple. Such variation is affected by many factors, ranging from the amount of flint available to the symbolism surrounding food preparation and consumption, which is itself linked to attitudes concerning body boundaries, culture/nature boundaries, and the like. Archaeologists have yet to consider the latter components in any detail.

Although Marxist approaches have an important contribution to make to an understanding of the relationships between techniques and society (Lemmonier 1983; 1984), the main concern in this chapter is to examine the contribution of Marxist archaeology to the understanding of social and ideological relations. In considering social structures in this context, the contrast with processual approaches again needs to be identified. In this chapter the term social structure does not mean the pattern of roles and relationships; rather it refers to the scheme of productive interactions which lies behind that pattern. However, my concern here is not to debate the full width of Marxist archaeology, which has been adequately covered elsewhere (Spriggs 1984; Trigger 1984). Rather, I wish briefly to outline the types of social structure that have been identified in Marxist archaeology, before considering Marxist archaeological discussions of ideology.

Marxist archaeology

Here we return to materialism, although some Marxist archaeologists would now claim to avoid the materialist/idealist split (Spriggs 1984). We shall see below that such claims can rarely be substantiated in archaeology, and the similarity with processual archaeology is clear in this respect. Rather, it is in the Marxist incorporation of the notion of structure that the major break with processual archaeology occurs. This is not to argue that Marxist archaeology avoids functional arguments, because we shall see below that it does not. What is new is an additional component, that all social practices involve dialectical relationships: the development of society occurs through the unity of opposites. Underlying the visible social system are relationships which embody incompatibilities, which are made compatible and which generate change. It is thus to the realm of contradiction and conflict that we must turn in order to assess the essence of Marxist archaeology.

The two main types of contradiction are those between the interests of social groups (as in the class struggle) and those between the forces and relations of production (to be defined below). In the first type of contradiction, an important emphasis in Marxism is on class divisions, in which a dominant class controls the means of production and appropriates surplus. The interests of the two classes are contradictory since the expansion of one class is at the expense of the other. This general notion has been applied in pre-capitalist societies, to social divisions based on age, sex, lineage and so on. Thus Faris (1983) suggests that in the Upper Palaeolithic in Europe men appropriated the products of the labour of women and maintained a position of dominance at the expense of women. The notion of 'structure' in such studies, although weakly developed, concerns the relations of production and appropriation that lie behind the apparent social relations (between men and women, chief and commoner etc.).

The second type of contradiction, clearly linked to and often underlying the first type, is structural incompatibility. Here the forces of production are in conflict with the relations of production. One view of these terms and their relationships is provided by Friedman (1974; see following diagram). The forces of production include the means of production (technology, the ecosystem: the means by which an environment is transformed into a product for man) and the organization of production (the organization of the labour force). The relations of production, on the other hand, are the social relations which correspond with the forces of production. These social relations will vary from society to society: for example, in some societies kinship orders the forces of production, whereas in the contemporary West it rarely does. The social relations of production organize the way in which the environment is to be used within the available technology; they also determine who works and how the product of labour is appropriated. In archaeology, as in other areas of Marxist analyses, major variation occurs in the relative importance given to the forces and relations of production. In some writings the forces of production appear to develop on their own, internally generated, leading to contradictions between the forces and relations of production. An example of this position is provided

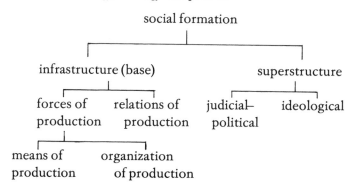

by Gilman's (1984) account of the Upper Palaeolithic Revolution. He argues that the Domestic Mode of Production (Sahlins 1972) characteristic of this period has internal contradictions: on the one hand local groups need external alliances in order to survive, but on the other hand they wish to maintain control of their own resources. More self-sufficient groups want to move out of the alliance network. As technology improves, each group becomes more self-sufficient and the contradiction between the alliance network and local production leads to bounded local alliances, which establish closed circles of mutual aid and limit obligations to assist others. Although Gilman claims (*ibid.*, p. 123) that technology does not specifically determine the social changes, and that the materialist determination is in the last, not the first, instance, the technological changes do appear primary (Fig. 5). They are generated as the result of the Darwinian selection of primary adaptive improvements in stone-tools (*ibid.*).

In such analyses contradictions between the forces and relations of production are generated by changes in the forces of production, and, as we shall see below, these contradictions lead to changes in the arena of style and ideology. Such viewpoints appear inadequate, particularly if one is interested in the reasons for technological change and the reasons for the precise form of the social relations. Thus many Marxists would now argue that, at least in pre-capitalist social formations, it is the social relations of production which either dominate or

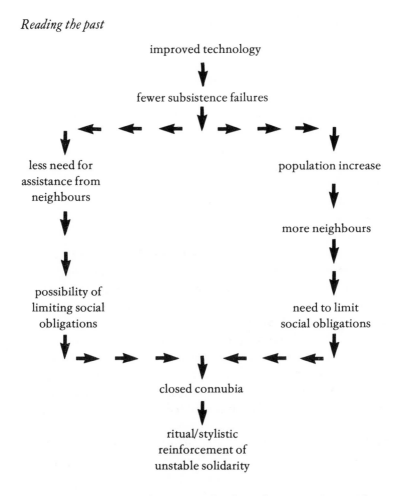

Fig. 5. The relation between technological improvements and social change over the course of the Upper Palaeolithic, as suggested by Gilman (1984).

are in a dialectical two-way relationship with the forces of production.

An interesting example of the view that the social relations dominate is provided by Bender's (1978) account of the adoption of agriculture. She suggests that prior to the adoption of farming local groups were competing for domination through rituals, feasting and exchange. It is these strategies of social dominance which lead to the need for increased local subsistence production and hence to more intensive production and the adoption of agriculture. Here changes in people's relationship with the environment, the forces of production, are dependent on social relations.

Such notions of the growth of dominance and ranking in initially egalitarian groups are outlined with clarity by Friedman (1975) and are developed and applied to the appearance of state societies by Friedman and Rowlands (1978). One aspect of Friedman's model, the prestige goods system, has now been widely applied in European prehistory (see for example Bradley 1984; Frankenstein and Rowlands 1978). In all such studies the social relations of production dominate, and ideology in particular plays a secondary role.

So far we have seen something of the concept of 'structure' in Marxist archaeology – that it concerns relations of production and appropriation. One of the reasons this structure is 'underlying', hidden from view, is that it is masked by ideology. We can now return to the main theme of this chapter: what is the role of ideology in relation to the social structure in Marxist archaeology?

Ideology

Archaeologists often make use of Marx's statement, made in 1859, that the superstructure, incorporating ideology, is founded on and arises from the infrastructure. Ideology then functions by masking the contradictions and conflicts within and between the forces and relations of production. Most Marxist archaeology has provided explanations in which ideology is determined by and functions in relation to the economy. While a reflexive relationship between base and superstructure is sometimes claimed, in practice applications have been largely materialist and functionalist (see below).

While, in the Marxist approach, ideology is explained by reference to its functions, there is a sense in which material culture is 'active'. As in the Wobst view (p. 26), material culture acts so that the system can work. However, on the whole this 'activity' is the fairly passive end-product of functional needs, even though these needs are rather different from those found in processual archaeology. The distinction is made clearly by Gilman (1984) in his Marxist reading of the Upper Palaeolithic transition, in contrast to that made by Wobst (1976). Rather than seeing Upper Palaeolithic style as functioning to facilitate cooperation within social groupings and to identify differences between them, Gilman argues that style and ritual develop because that cooperation incorporates inherent contradictions. The desire to break out of alliance networks and concentrate on retaining production within local groups leads to unstable closed connubia. Thus style and ritual help to create social groupings which would otherwise be continually breaking down. Material culture here functions by providing a masking ideology, hiding or misrepresenting the internal contradictions.

Another important Upper Palaeolithic analysis which incorporates a symbolic structure which ideologically 'hides' social conflict is carried out by Faris (1983). Faris notes a contrast between western European Palaeolithic wall painting and mobiliary art. The parietal art mainly depicts big game animals which require a lot of skill in hunting. The art itself is skilled and must have involved considerable effort, including the construction of scaffolding in some places. In contrast, plants and small animals, although these are known from archaeological deposits to be an important part of the diet, are not depicted. Female figurines, on the other hand, misrepresent reality in another way. In this mobiliary art, it is the mid-body sexual and reproductive parts that are emphasized at the expense of arms and facial features – the image is not of a working body. In the art as a whole, then, it is male hunting activities that are emphasized, even though such activities probably only produced a portion of the resources consumed. Small animals and plants and female production are not represented; the woman appears only as reproductive.

Faris is careful to identify his own perception biasses in this reconstruction. But here both symbolic form and content are

examined. The structure of signs misrepresents the role played
by women in society – in other words the symbolism acts ideologically to transform the relations of production. Male dominance is based on the appropriation of female labour, and the
cave wall art mystifies the contradiction and prevents conflict.
Material culture has to be understood both as part of an
aesthetic tradition, and as part of an ideology within social
strategies of domination.

In both of the above studies of the Upper Palaeolithic,
ideology is interpreted functionally in relation to the economic
base (the forces and the social relations of production). A
further example is provided by Kristiansen (1984) in his study
of the role of ideology in the construction of megalithic burial
in Neolithic Europe. His aim is to determine how ideological
and cultural norms correspond to their material functions of
reproduction (*ibid.*, p. 77). The megalithic monuments are
seen as representing a ritualized extension of production
organized through the communal lineage structure. Surplus
production for lineage leaders is transformed into ritual feasting and ancestor worship.

In Kristiansen's study, the materialism is clear, but it should
also be noted that the social reality against which the ideology
is compared can only be accessed archaeologically through the
ideology itself – that is, through interpretations of the burial
monuments. Thus, as with the processual studies discussed in
chapter 2, the materialism is more apparent than real. It is
certainly not possible to determine the ideology from the
material base since the material base is only known through
the ideology.

A further characteristic of Kristiansen's study is that the
ideology is the conscious world of ritual. Other studies, such
as that of Leone (1984), have concentrated more on the ideological aspects of the unconscious taken-for-granteds that are
inherent in all aspects of life (Althusser 1977). For Leone,
these 'givens' – ideas about nature, cause, time, person – serve
to naturalize and mask inequalities in the social order. Ideology disguises the arbitrariness of social relations of production,
making them appear resident in nature or the past and thus

inevitable. Leone focusses in particular on the layout of an
eighteenth-century garden, recovered by historical archaeologists, in Annapolis, Maryland. In the eighteenth century,
social control by plantation owners was being weakened in a
number of ways, and wealthy members of the planter-gentry,
such as William Paca, the owner of the Annapolis garden, held
contradictory beliefs, on the one hand basing his substantial
inherited wealth in part on slavery and on the other hand
passionately defending liberty. To mask this contradiction,
Leone suggests that Paca's position of power was placed within
nature. The ideal of Georgian order in the house and the carefully laid out garden conform to rules of bilateral symmetry
and perspective. In this way the arbitrariness of the social order
is naturalized, and the gentry is isolated and distanced from
attack on the established order. The balance and organization
of the garden appear convincingly natural and ordered, thus
making the elite the natural centre of social control.

In this example, once again, the materialist conception of
ideology is clear – the ideology functions in relation to growing contradictions within eighteenth-century society. But the
important contribution of such studies to the concerns in this
volume as outlined in chapter 1, are that an attempt is made to
examine the way in which structures of symbolic meaning may
relate to social structures and systems. In Leone's example we
are back with symbolic structures, but now these are linked to
social structures via ideological and social processes. As we
saw in chapter 3, in structuralist archaeology such linkages are
not the central focus of concern.

I wish to use Leone's convincing account of the role of
material culture in ideology (for further examples see Miller
and Tilley 1984) in order to begin a four-point critique of
ideology as discussed in Marxist archaeology.

First criticism

It often appears in the Marxist analyses that the ideology is
shared by all in society – thus, once again, aspects of a normative view are retained (see p. 8). All in Annapolis view the garden in the same way and get the same sense of order and

nature out of it. An equivalent criticism can be made of all the examples discussed in this chapter. There is no indication anywhere that the same material culture may have different meanings and different ideological effects for different social groups.

Indeed, the extent to which people are duped by the ideas of the dominant class is remarkable in these accounts. For Leone, the ordering of architecture, street plans, rows of trees, the training of gardens, disguise the arbitrariness of the social order. It may be true that the ruling classes themselves believe their own ideology, but no evidence is provided that all members of society make these linkages between garden layout and social order or that they in any way value or respect the garden. As Giddens (1979, p. 72) points out, 'a good case can be made to the effect that only dominant class groups have ever been strongly committed to dominant ideologies'. One must not overestimate the degree of conviction with which all members of society (subordinate and even dominant) accept symbol-systems. Subordinate groups within society often have their own views in relation to their own interests, views which may be covert because of the control by authorities of the dominant modes of discourse. But if we wish to introduce the individual as an active social agent, as outlined in chapter 1, we must allow that individuals have some ability to penetrate ideologies and to have independent opinions of their own conditions of existence.

Second criticism

A second, closely related point concerns the tendency in all Marxist archaeology to oppose ideology and the social reality, the 'real' conditions of existence, the 'real' contradictions. As we have seen, ideologies are described as naturalizing or masking inequalities in the social order; but 'inequality' is itself a value-laden term and can be described as ideological. The Marxist notion of false-consciousness implies that people cannot see the reality of their existence because that reality is hidden from them by ideologies. But what *is* the social reality?

For many Marxist archaeologists the social reality is defined

as the forces and relations of production. But Marxism then
has to face its own critique, that Marxist definition of the
social reality is itself ideological. Since reality has to be perceived and created by the observer, it is itself ideology. To
take the position that Marxism offers the one true science that
can identify objective reality is simply to state a belief.

As we have seen in discussing Kristiansen's study, the problem of the definition of social reality is particularly acute in
archaeology since material culture serves as both social reality
and ideology. Thus the lineage mode of appropriation of surplus may be identified from burial, but the same burial monuments are interpreted as ideologies masking social reality.
Where, then, is the social reality?

For different social actors, the social inequalities and contradictions may have different 'realities'. For Althusser (1977),
whose work has been discussed in archaeology most fully by
Shanks and Tilley (1982), ideology is not distorted communication, but is functionally necessary in all societies. Rather
than opposing ideology and reality, Althusser seeks to express
ideology as the practical unconscious organization of the day-
to-day. But it is particularly Foucault's discussion of power as
ever-present, a constituent of all social action, that has come
to the fore in recent archaeological debate (Miller and Tilley
1984). In *Surveillir et punir* Foucault (1977) shows that power is
not simply repressive, negative; it is also positive, productive
of knowledge. It does not just mask, conceal, repress – it also
produces reality. Power is not a general system of domination
exerted by one group over another. Rather, power is every-
where, produced at every moment in every action. It is present
in the ideal as much as in the material. One can argue that
there is an unceasing struggle in which power relations are
transformed, strengthened and sometimes reversed by the
manipulation of symbolic and material capital, the two being
fully interdependent and difficult to distinguish.

Following the direction of Foucault, Miller and Tilley (*ibid.*)
define power as the capacity to transform, and they make a
distinction between *power to* and *power over*. Rather than oppos-

ing ideology to reality, they relate it to interest. Actors have interests by being members of groups, and to examine ideology is to see how symbolic meanings are mobilized to legitimate the sectional interests of those groups. Following Giddens (1979; 1981), there are three ways in which ideologies function: (1) the representation of sectional interests as universal, (2) the denial or transmutation of contradictions, and (3) the naturalization of the present, or reification. These ideas have immediate implications for archaeologists (Hodder 1982c; Miller and Tilley 1984). For example, if burial remains are seen as ideological naturalizations of the social order, then burial variability within cemeteries (how the bones are laid out, the contents of the graves, and so on) will correlate directly with the structure of the society, but if burial remains in a particular society deny contradictions, then the archaeological burial data cannot be used to 'read off' the social organization. Material culture, then, is a type of social reality, but it is not the only type.

Different sectional interests in society develop their own ideologies in relation to other ideologies and interests. Social interests and power relations can be seen from many different points of view within the same society. Interest and power can be defined in terms other than the control over labour and material resources. Different ideologies coexist in relation to each other and the dominant ideology is continually being subverted from other points of view. Any arena of material culture use (domestic, ritual, exchange, burial) frequently involves the negotiation of these different meanings/powers in relation to each other. What may be seen by one group as an inequality on one dimension may be seen as an equality on another. William Paca's garden may have worked well for William Paca, legitimating his own social interests, but whether anyone else was taken in by it is less clear. It could be argued that a material culture statement of this type was socially divisive. Indeed all ideologies that appear to 'mask', in the process 'reveal'.

Third criticism

The third criticism of Marxist approaches to ideology is that the cross-cultural method applied usually pays insufficient regard to the specific historical context. It is easy to apply Giddens' three types of ideology in a wide range of circumstances. In the examples discussed in this chapter, notions of prestige, naturalization, masking and so on are applied with little attempt to see if the cross-cultural model is appropriate. In Leone's example, how do we know the garden acts ideologically in the way described? We are told little of the context of use: how is the garden used, do subordinate groups ever visit or even see the garden, do subordinate groups use such ordering in their own homes and gardens on a smaller scale or are their gardens very different, and so on?

Equally, the cross-cultural emphasis leads to an inability to account for the specificity of ideological forms. Thus in Gilman's analysis, the general interpretation of style and ritual as ideology does nothing to explain why cave art is found as opposed to other ritual. In relation to Faris' study, it is informative to ask, why does cave wall art not occur in central Europe in the Upper Palaeolithic, despite the existence of appropriate caves? The generalized reference to ideological functions does little to account for such differences. Equally, there are many ways in which William Paca could have projected a sense of order.

Fourth criticism

A final limitation of Marxist approaches to ideology concerns the generation and generative role of ideology. The inability to explain the specificity of ideology (third criticism) is associated with an inability to explain its 'becoming'. Certainly, the ideologies come about to achieve a function, but can it really be claimed that the ideological need to mask appropriation by lineage heads leads to megalithic burial monuments, or that a need to legitimate social control in Annapolis leads to an organized garden? The poverty of stimulus argument is here at work, throwing doubt on the ability of Marxist analysis to explain both the specificity of ideology (third criticism) and its generation (fourth criticism). These criticisms are very similar to those made in chapters 2 and 3. As in all the other approaches described so far in this book, one is left with the question, where does the particular ideology (structure, ideational sub-system or whatever) come from?

Since the specificity and 'becoming' of ideology have not been approached in Marxist archaeological analyses, so too there has been little attempt to show how the ideology itself determines and creates society. Since the emphasis has been on the functioning of ideologies, and because of the materialist bent of such analyses, the reflexive role of ideology has been little discussed. For example, the Georgian order manifest in Paca's house and garden is seen by Leone as appropriate for the needed social functions, but ideals concerning the organization of space and time, which Leone identifies in the garden, are themselves part of a long historical tradition which harks back to the Classical civilizations of the Mediterranean world. It would be possible to argue that this Classical ideal of order has itself played a part in generating Western society and in determining the social interests to which Paca aspired – in other words, we could give a more creative and active role to ideology, and to material culture as ideological.

Ideology: conclusions

Ideology, then, is an aspect of symbol-systems. It refers to that component of symbol-systems most closely involved in the negotiation of power from varying points of interest within society. Cultural meanings and symbols are used within strategies of power and in the negotiation of control, but they also partly form those strategies. Ideology cannot be opposed to social relations of production. It cannot be explained as functioning in relation to some social reality, because that reality, and the analysis of the relationship between ideology and reality, are themselves ideological. Rather, ideology is the framework within which, from a particular standpoint, resources are given value, inequalities are defined and power is legitimated. Ideas are themselves the 'real' resources used in the negotiation of power; and material resources are themselves parts of the ideological apparatus.

To study ideology thus involves two components for which archaeologists are theoretically ill-equipped. First, since ideologies cannot be measured in terms of objective conditions and functions, they must be studied 'from the inside', on their own terms. These terms of reference are historically generated. We need methods, then, for getting 'inside' the principles of meaning through which societies are generated. This problem will be addressed in chapter 5.

Second, critical analysis of Marxist archaeology leads back to the importance of the self-monitoring individual, who, as we have seen in previous chapters, has been left out of all archaeological approaches and theories. Equally, the emphasis has shifted from the functions that the individual performs and from the uses of the products which he/she fashions, to the generation of action. But how do individuals act in the world? We have seen that the standard answer in archaeology has been to say that individuals are rule-bound. In systems archaeology the rules of the regulative system or the roles in society determine individual action. In structuralism, the individual is controlled by universals of the human mind or by generative structures which are played out beyond his/her reference. In Marxist archaeology the individual is driven by material conditions or structural incompatibilities and is mystified by dominant ideologies. If we reject rule-bound behaviour as an adequate description of human action and material culture production, where then do we go? To consider this question is the task of the following section.

Practice and structuration

In outlining a 'theory of practice', Bourdieu (1977) notes the difference between, on the one hand, observing and analysing social events, and, on the other hand, participating in activities.

Structuralism, for example, allows us to see how pattern is generated, but gives us no indication of how we make relevant use of structures in constantly changing situations. Giddens (1979; 1981) is also concerned to escape notions of change which involve the playing out of some pre-set code.

Both Bourdieu and Giddens thus develop theories of practice or social action, called by Giddens 'structuration', in which there is a recursive relationship between structure and practice. Bourdieu's account is of particular relevance to archaeologists because he develops his theory in relation to material culture and the use of space. Indeed his ideas have been applied in ethnoarchaeology by, for example, Donley (1982), Moore (1982) and Braithwaite (1982), and in archaeology by Barrett (1981) and Davis (1984).

Bourdieu situates his notion of *habitus* (singular and plural) between structure and practice. The habitus are defined as systems of

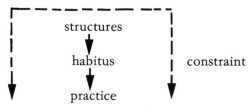

durable but transposable dispositions, including, for example, a sense of honour, but also left/right, up/down and other structuring principles. The habitus are strategy generating principles enabling agents to cope with unforeseen situations. Rather than seeing habitus as abstract sets of mechanistic rules in a filing cabinet in the mind, Bourdieu emphasizes the importance of practical logic and knowledge. All the schemes of categorization and perception are included, but the habitus is unconscious, a linguistic and cultural competence. In day-to-day activities, there is a practical mastery involving tact, dexterity and savoir faire which cannot be reduced to rules. In the same vein, Giddens suggests that the knowledgeability of lay actors, which mediates between structure and practice, includes both discursive and practical consciousness. Practical consciousness involves knowledge of 'how to go on' in society – it is skilled, an artistry in day-to-day activity, varied and strategic, dependent on context. Individuals reflexively monitor their actions and can penetrate or gain an understanding of the structures of society. Regular patterns of behaviour occur as a result of practices generated through habitus, but there are few norms and rigid rules, except insofar as these are abstracted and intellectualized, by onlookers. For actors, behaviour is context dependent, strategic and practical.

Nevertheless a commonality of behaviour does occur within social groups. 'It is because each agent has the means of acting as a judge of others and of himself that custom has hold of him' (Bourdieu 1977, p. 17). Through judgement and assessment of the effects of what the self and others have done, there is a tendency towards a consensus of meaning, harmonization of experiences and homogeneity of habitus. Judgement and value are inseparable from sectional interests within the process of group formation and maintenance.

Bourdieu also considers how the habitus is passed from generation to generation without going through discourse or consciousness. The central position of processes of enculturation in Bourdieu's theory is of importance for archaeology because it links social practices with the 'culture history' of society. As the habitus is passed down through time it plays an active role in social action and is transformed in those actions. This recursiveness, Giddens' 'duality of structure', is possible because the habitus is a *practical* logic.

The schemes of the habitus are passed down from practice to practice, but this does not mean that learning is a mechanistic remembering of appropriate actions. In the daily pattern of life, in proverbs, songs, riddles, games, watching adults and interacting with them, a child has no difficulty in grasping the rationale behind the series of events. The child adjusts and accommodates subjective and objective patterns, patterns 'in here' and 'out there', giving rise to systematic dispositions. The habitus which results is based on the child's own social position as he/she sees how others react to him/her. In particular, the house, and the use of space and objects in a house, lead a child to an understanding of the habitus. The ' "book" from which the children learn their vision of the world is read with the body' (*ibid.*, p. 90), in moving through space, from 'male' to 'female' parts of the house, from 'light' to 'dark' and so on. The same home then comes to be perceived differently by different social groups, through their different habitus. Donley (1982) provides an elegant example of how in Kenyan Swahili houses, men and women learn their place in the world through the use of space and objects in the house. It is the practices, in the process of enculturation, that act back on the habitus, so that Bourdieu can talk of 'the mind born of the world of objects' (*ibid.*, p. 91).

Bourdieu's theory of practice presents an implicit invitation to archaeologists to come to an understanding of the principles lying behind other cultural practices through an examination of and involvement in objects arranged in space and in contexts of use. In the same way that the child absorbs the principles of action, so the archaeologist can 'read' the surviving 'book', without necessary reference to abstract or spoken meanings. I shall return later to the implications of this realization for archaeological 'theory' and for the public presentation of archaeology.

The potential offered by Bourdieu's insight is considerable. It is exciting to realize that mundane items in the material world, of the type excavated by archaeologists – pots, bones, pins and door-frames – can all play a part in the process of enculturation, in forming the social world. Through practical enculturation it is possible to instill 'a whole cosmology, an ethic, a metaphysic, a political philosophy, through injunctions as insignificant as "stand up straight" or "don't hold your knife in your left hand" ' (Bourdieu, *ibid.*, p. 94). 'Stand up straight', for example, may relate, in the particular cultural associations of straightness (such as straight male spears) to valued notions of 'talking straight', 'being straight', as opposed to being bent over, submissive. A whole philosophy of male dominance is thus taken for granted. Every mundane pot and scratched decoration, every pig and cow skull, is in this way the node of a network of associations and oppositions which tell us about the way the world is put together.

Both Bourdieu and Giddens link structuralism and Marxism, and outline a theory of practice of considerable importance in archaeology. Their concern is to avoid both objectivism (social action happens with mechanical inevitability, through processes of which actors are ignorant) and subjectivism (social action is produced solely by skilled actors). Rather, there is a duality of structure: the structure is both the medium and outcome of action. The individual plays a central role as self-monitoring, creative and with degrees of competence. Material culture in particular plays a highly active role, creating society and creating continual change.

Shanks and Tilley (1982) concentrate on one of Bourdieu's areas of practical knowledge – the use of the body as a map or framework by which people 'live through' their habitus. The world is known through the body, unconsciously. Within the body there is a variety of possible whole/part relations. Disarticulated human bone remains from Neolithic tombs in Britain and Sweden were found to have been grouped into piles showing body/limb, upper limb/lower limb, right/left distinctions. The body symmetry is then seen as naturalizing contradictions in society, for example between social control by lineage heads and socialized production. The symmetry between body parts is a denial of asymmetrical relations in life.

Although in this example a sophisticated account is given of the relationship between structure and practice, with the role of the individual considered, some of the limitations that have been encountered in other studies remain, particularly in relation to contextual meanings and history. As in other studies influenced by the work of Bourdieu and Giddens (see the articles in Hodder 1982c) particular historical meanings are not taken into account; the approach remains largely cross-cultural and 'from the outside'. Thus Shanks and Tilley do not examine whether there are other realms of evidence in Neolithic society in Britain and Sweden which show left/right symmetries, nor what these symmetries might represent there. Childe argued for Neolithic Orkney (Hodder 1982a) that a right/left division of huts might relate to male/female on the basis of artifacts and bed sizes. I have also argued (Hodder 1984a) that the Neolithic tombs 'mean' houses found elsewhere in central Europe where they played an important part in male/female relationships. If further work could establish the relevance of such contexts, the bone organization in the tombs might be shown to have had specific meanings in the male/female negotiation of power and authority, rather than being related to the types of power relations described by Shanks and Tilley.

Without consideration of the content of meaning in a culture-historical context (what do left/right, burial tombs etc. mean in Neolithic Britain and Sweden?) it becomes impossible to explain the ideological functions of symbol-systems. Equally it is impossible to explain why any *particular* symbol-system was employed, how it came about. For example, the ideo-logical analysis of the Neolithic tombs cannot explain why the same monuments are not commonly found in central Europe, where similar structural contradictions can be presumed. Shanks and Tilley's elegant and innovative analysis of one type of habitus needs to be tied to careful consideration of historical and contextual meanings.

Indeed, this last point is one that has come up throughout this chapter, and throughout this book so far. Processual, structuralist and Marxist analyses all seem limited in their ability adequately to explain the past, because they refuse to grapple with the content of historical meanings and with the question of where the style, structure or ideology comes from. How can we explain how a tomb functions adaptively in society if we do not know what it means? How can we interpret bi-lateral symmetry or horizontal zonation without understand-ing the historical meanings of such structures, the elements used in them, and the contexts (for example pots) on which they occur? How can we suggest what is being naturalized by left/right symmetries without knowing their meaning content?

We have got some way with the initial programme. Archae-ology has been broadened by structuralism and Marxism to include studies of the structure of meaning and of the active involvement of such structures in social change. In the search for an adequate account of material culture as meaningfully constituted, there is now a growing tendency in the literature to examine the structure and the functions (both in an adaptive, processual sense, and in a Marxist sense) of material symbols. Yet all the approaches examined so far are distinctive in that they fail to deal adequately and explicitly with the content of historical meanings.

5 Archaeology and history

In this chapter it will be argued that archaeology should recapture its traditional links with history. Unfortunately the term 'history' is used with a variety of different meanings by different people, and it is first necessary to establish what I do and do not mean by the word here. I do not mean the explanation of change by reference to antecedent events; simply to describe a series of events leading up to a particular moment in time is a travesty of the historical method. Neither do I mean that phase n is dependent on phase n-1. Many types of archaeology involve such a dimension. Thus many social evolutionary theories expect some dependence in the moves between bands, tribes, chiefdoms or states, or in the adoption of agriculture (Woodburn 1980). In the application of Darwinian-type arguments, the selection of a new social form is constrained by the existing 'gene-pool'. In systems theory the 'trajectory' of a system is dependent on prior conditions and system states. Each trajectory may be historically unique and specific in content, but general laws of system functioning can be applied. Within Marxism the resolution of conflict and contradiction is emergent in the pre-existing system, as part of the dialectical process of history.

History, in all such work, involves a particularist dimension, but it also involves explaining the move from phase n-1 to n according to a set of universal rules. As such, the historian remains on the *outside* of events, as a natural scientist records experimental data. But history in the sense intended here involves also getting at the *inside* of events, at the intentions and thoughts of subjective actors. The historian talks of 'actions', not behaviour, movements or events. Collingwood (1946, p. 213) provides an example. Historians do not just record that Caesar crossed a river called the Rubicon on a certain date – they talk of Caesar's defiance of Republican law.

This book began with the question, how do we get at past

cultural meanings? We have gone to and from materialism and back again. Throughout, the core of the reconstructions attempted within any 'ism' has been seen to be based on weakly developed arguments about cultural meaning. Within the materialist systemic–processual approach, it was assumed that, for example, burial is for social display, so that in conditions of challenged norms of succession burials will reflect status rivalry (p. 24). To interpret the function of burials in this way we must make assumptions about what they meant to the people at the time. Equally, a head-dress can only mark social affili-ation (p. 24) if it is perceived by those involved to have had meaning in these terms. It might be counter-argued that, what-ever the artifacts meant, they still had the suggested functions. Yet it is difficult to see how an artifact can have a social func-tion (such as burial for social display) if the meaning is not appropriate to the function (as when death or material accumu-lation comes to be seen as 'dirty', 'uncultured').

As a result of this inadequate approach to meaning we turned in chapter 3 to structuralism, but here it was found that mean-ing content was often imposed without care. Units of analysis were defined *a priori*, symbols were given meanings (male or female for example), and asymmetries were interpreted (as 'organic' for example). The structuralist method itself pro-vided few guidelines as to how one might reconstruct the sub-jective meanings in which the structures are built.

So we return to materialism. In chapter 4 it was shown that in most Marxist analyses of material culture it is again the functions that are examined (to mask social reality etc.) rather than the meaning content. Even approaches that have devel-oped a sophisticated non-functional theory of social action and material practice, have still failed, in relation to archae-ological data, adequately to examine meaning content.

Even within approaches not discussed in this book, subjec-tive meanings are assumed in the minds of people long dead. For example, the economy of a prehistoric site is often recon-structed on the basis of bone residues (chapter 1, p. 13). But to assume that bones discarded on a settlement bear any relation to the economy is to make assumptions about how people perceived animals, bones, discard etc. In many societies complex social meanings are attached to domestic animals, bones and dirt. To assume that the bones are not transformed culturally is to assume that 'they' had attitudes not so dissimilar to 'ours'. As a further example, if I say that the population at a certain site was probably about 'x', there is hidden in this statement a reconstruction of meanings in the minds of people long dead. Since I cannot directly 'see' the population in the past, I have to infer it from, for example, settlement space. Of course I can bolster my argument with cross-cultural evidence. But even if we could show that all societies today have a predictable relationship between population size and settlement area (which we cannot – see Hodder 1982d), to use such information to interpret the past is still to make assumptions about peoples' attitudes to space in that particular historical context. How much space individuals or groups need or think they need for certain activities is, at least partly, a question of symbolism, meaning and intention. As Collingwood (1939, p. 133) and Taylor (1948) noted, it is almost impossible even to describe archaeological data without some interpretative terms implying purpose, like 'wall', 'pottery', 'implement', 'hearth'. While Neolithic polished stone axes were thought to be thunderbolts their utilitarian functions (to cut down Neolithic trees) could not be elucidated by mere analysis. It is only when we make assumptions about the subjective meanings in the minds of people long dead that we can begin to do archaeology.

Throughout the approaches described in this book there has been a refusal to face this unhappy situation directly. Archaeologists have preferred to avoid the problem, and have grasped the comfort of empirical science, a cracked and broken facade. We must now face the subjectivity of meaning directly.

I take it to be the role of history to understand human action, rather than event. To get at action is to get at subjective meanings, at the *inside* of events. There is thus a close link between history and idealism. By idealism I do not mean a view that the material world does not exist: rather, the term as defined earlier (p. 18), suggests that the material world is as it appears. It has to be perceived before it can be acted upon. Historical idealism is then the study of how these subjective meanings come about in historical contexts; but since history has itself been defined in terms of getting at action (which involves belief) and the *inside* of events, the term historical idealism is largely redundant in the present context.

There are two aspects of history that I want to discuss in this chapter. First, I wish to look at ways in which subjective meanings are regenerated over the long term in relation to practice. Second, the historical method itself will be examined.

History of the long term

The usual way in which archaeologists discuss developments over long spans of time is to divide up their data into phases and to discuss the reasons for change between the phases. History is thus a discontinuous process, whether the approach being followed is culture-historical (when the discontinuities are invasions and so on), processual (systemic, adaptive change) or Marxist (change from contradiction and crisis). As we have seen (p. 49), structuralism does not cope well with change.

While attempts have been made within these approaches to blur the edges between phases (see for example Higgs and Jarman 1969), there is little notion of history as a continuous process, and few archaeologists have attempted to reconstruct the way in which subjective, contextual meanings are related to practice over the long term. If we want to understand the subjective orientations of people at one moment in time, in order to understand their society (or ours), how far back do we have to go? Do the meanings change, but always in relation to what went before, as a continuous process?

Almost by definition, those who are interested in the continuity of cultural meanings over the long term tend to be interested in the particular. If each phase is to be explained separately, in comparison with other societies, the unique historical development is played down. But for those interested in cultural meanings, cross-cultural generalities have to be proved, not assumed, so emphasis is placed on understanding the particular in its own terms. We have already seen (p. 77) that all archaeology is concerned with the particular historical context to some degree, and Trigger (1978) has shown that, on the other hand, history involves generalization. But in both archaeological and non-archaeological studies it is particularist studies combined with a concern for the 'inside' of events which have led to the most profound and far-reaching statements on the nature of the relationships between meaning and practice.

An important study of such relationships over the long term is Max Weber's (1976; first published in 1904–5) analysis of the relationship between the Protestant ethic and the spirit of capitalism. Although this is not an archaeological example, I intend to discuss it at some length for reasons which will become clear below. Weber begins with a particular problem to which he gives a particular answer. His question is 'why does capitalism emerge in western Europe and not in other parts of the world?' Some form of capitalism existed, he suggests, in China, India, Babylon, but the particular ethos or spirit found in Europe, which laid the basis for the modern capitalist ethic, was lacking. Weber identifies this ethic as 'one's duty in a calling', whatever that profession might be. Rational conduct on the basis of the idea of the calling could be linked to other specific and peculiar forms of rationalism found in Western culture, as seen in music, law and administration as well as in the economic system.

Weber suggests that the distinctive character of Western capitalism is linked to (though not in any direct sense caused by) the rise of various forms of ascetic Protestantism, especially Calvinism. Data are quoted which show that business leaders, owners of capital and skilled and technical grades of labour are overwhelmingly Protestant in western European countries of mixed religious composition. Catholic traditionalism was authoritarian and did not sanction the pursuit of gain at the expense of others; its greater 'other-worldliness' inhibited capitalist enterprise. Calvinism, however, sanctioned 'this-worldly' asceticism. Individuals were born into an apparently unalterable order of things, and predestination led a person to 'do the works of him who sent him, as long as it is yet day' (Weber 1976, p. 156).

In his analysis Weber is specifically arguing against Marxist historical materialism in which the forces and relations of production are primary. Not that he ignores such factors or even thinks they are unimportant, but he wishes to give equal weight to an idealist notion, that an historically specific set of ideas influences the way people organize their society and economy. His concern is to examine the subjective meaning-complex of action and to emphasize that 'rationality' is subjective, in relation to particular 'ends' or 'givens'. He suggests that every artifact can be understood only in terms of the meaning which its production and use have had or will have for human action.

The Protestant asceticism is seen as developing over long stretches of time, and as being regenerated through enculturation so that it becomes taken for granted. Ultimately the formation of rational jurisprudence inherited from Roman law played a role in the development of a specific Western type of rationalism. The origins of the capitalist spirit can be traced back to a time previous to the advent of capitalism (p. 54), and the Puritan emphasis on continuous bodily or mental labour is partly derived from the fact that 'labour is . . . an approved ascetic technique, as it always has been in the Western Church, in sharp contrast not only to the Orient but to almost all monastic rules the world over' (p. 163).

But Weber does not see this set of ideas developing on its own. Rather, the material and the ideal are integrated, so that to explain each action or social product it is necessary to consider both the historical context of subjective meanings and the practice of daily life. The religious ideas change partly through debate amongst religious leaders, but also in relation to, but not dominated by, the totality of social conditions, especially economic ones (p. 183). Richard Baxter, a writer on Puritan ethics, 'continually adjusted to the practical experiences of his own ministerial activity' so that his dogma changed in relation to practical activity (p. 156). Weber continually notes the difference between philosophers and religious ideals ver-

sus 'the layman', 'the practical', and 'the average'. Under
Calvinism 'The moral conduct of the average man was thus
deprived of its planless and unsystematic character [that it had
in Catholicism] and subjected to a consistent method for conduct as a whole' (p. 117).

The spirit of capitalism was born from the spirit of Christian
asceticism. The dogma went into everyday life, began to dominate worldly morality, and played its part in building the modern economic order. However, the practical consequences may
be unintended. Thus the religious reformers of Calvinism and
other Puritan sects were concerned to save souls; the pursuit
of worldly goods was not an end in itself. The purely religious
motives had cultural and social consequences which were unforeseen and even unwished for (pp. 89–90). The results were
often far-removed from and even in contradiction to all that
the religious reformers were trying to attain.

We see, then, in Weber's account, the dialectical relationships between theory and practice, between idea and material,
and the same emphases on social action (purposeful behaviour),
unintended consequences and contradictions that were identified in the preceding chapter. Here however, because a *long*
historical context is provided, the equal contribution of ideals
and values is identified. In the short term, in the instant of
action, Bourdieu's habitus appears dominated by the conditions of existence, but over the long term, and in contrast
with other historical sequences, the social and economic conditions are themselves seen to be generated within sets of cultural meanings.

Through time, Weber records, the relative dominance of
religious ideas and the social economy varies. Initially, the
ascetic tendency of Puritanism led to social action and allowed
the further development of an economic system, forms of
which already had been in existence. Certain aspects of capitalist business organization are considerably older than the Refor-
mation (p. 91), but it was the religious changes which allowed
the new economic order to develop. In addition, Puritanism
was 'anti-authoritarian', leading to fanatical opposition of the
Puritans to the ordinances of the British monarch (p. 167).

So, at first, 'the Puritan wanted to work in a calling', and religion directed the capitalist enterprise, but now 'we are forced to do so' (p. 181). Through time the rational order became bound to the technical and economic conditions of machine production. Today these material conditions 'determine the lives of all the individuals who are born into the mechanism' (p. 181), and the religious basis has been lost.

I have discussed Weber's account at some length, because, while I cannot remember ever having seen a reference to Weber in archaeological texts (which is itself extraordinary if it reflects a real lack of such references), his work contains many of the aspects of historical interpretation for which this book searches. There is a full consideration of subjective, contextual meanings, an account of how these meanings develop and can be understood in their own historical terms, and the location of the individual in society. Weber argues against functionally deterministic relationships, and sees individual action as the building block of social totalities. The social whole is full of tensions, divisions, and contradictions, and individuals variously interpret the world(s) in which they live.

Despite the emphases on the subjective and specific, Weber does not lapse into sceptical relativism and particularism – he thinks that it is possible to understand other people's subjectivity. One need not have been Caesar in order to understand Caesar. The mind can grasp other contexts and other meanings, as long as it pieces together the 'spirit' of other times from individual segments of historical reality rather than imposing the formula from outside (p. 47). Equally, having carried out such detailed interpretation, generalization is possible both within historical contexts and between them.

As Giddens (1976) points out, much of Weber's data and interpretation have since been questioned. It has not been my concern here to demonstrate the validity of Weber's account, but to use the example to show how consideration of historical meanings, over the long term and in contrast to historical developments in other parts of the world, points to the inadequacy of materialist and objectivist accounts and emphasizes the importance of the subjective and particular.

While Weber's account already provides some indication of the relationship between idea and practice, it is perhaps Sahlins (1981) who provides the clearest example of the way in which the types of approaches outlined by Bourdieu and Giddens (see chapter 4) can be applied to the long term. While I will provide an ethnohistoric example of my own in chapter 6, it is of value to consider briefly the way in which Sahlins demonstrates the links between structure, habitus and practice.

In Hawaii, Sahlins recognizes sets of preconceptions and ideas which are part of action. For example, *mana* is a creative force that renders visible the invisible, that gives meaning to goodness and godliness. The divine *mana* of chiefs is manifest in their brilliance, their shining, like the sun. On the daily level, such notions orientate actions, as habitus, but they are changed in practice, in 'structures of the conjuncture'. No-one can ever know exactly how a particular event or meeting will be played out in practice. The intended and unintended consequences of action lead to reformulation of the habitus and of the social structure.

More clearly, at moments of culture contact, as when Cook came to Hawaii, two opposing habitus come into conflict in practice and radical change may ensue. Sahlins shows how, on their arrival in Hawaii, Cook and the Europeans were perceived within traditional frameworks, were seen to have *mana*. But in the playing out of practical scenes from different viewpoints (Hawaiian and European), unintended consequences rebounded back on these perceptions, causing contradictions and conflict. Ultimately Cook was killed as part of these processes, and *mana* became transferred to all things British, leading to social reordering within Hawaii.

There is much in this example which relates to Weber's accounts, but the more detailed work and greater awareness of the problem of the relationship between structure and practice leads to a fuller understanding of how society and economy are embedded within subjective meanings but are yet able to act back and change those meanings.

Where can we look in archaeology to find any aspects of such studies? As we have seen, direct influence from Weber (or from Sahlins' recent work on Hawaii) is difficult to find. But in the early part of this century, Childe envisioned his purpose in writing *The Dawn of European Civilisation* (first edition 1925) to be the understanding of the particular nature of European culture and the identification of the origin of that spirit of independence and inventiveness that led to the industrial revolution. Indeed his purpose was remarkably similar to that of Weber. He suggested that the distinctively European spirit began in the Bronze Age.

Childe claimed that, despite diffusion from the Orient, Europe adopted and improved methods and techniques with a vitality which contrasted with the traditionalism and authoritarianism of Eastern civilizations. Bronze Age Crete in particular was essentially modern in outlook: 'The Minoan spirit was thoroughly European and in no sense oriental' (1925, p. 2). Unlike Egypt and Mesopotamia, there are in Crete no stupendous palaces, gigantic temples, tombs and pyramids, and this absence shows the lack of autocratic power and despotism. Equally the art in Crete was neither formal nor conservative, but it had

> the modern naturalism, the truly occidental feeling for life and nature that distinguish Minoan vase paintings, frescoes and intaglios. Beholding these charming scenes of games and processions, animals and fishes, flowers and trees we breathe already a European atmosphere. Likewise in industry the absence of the unlimited labour-power at the disposal of a despot necessitated a concentration on the invention and elaboration of tools and weapons that foreshadows the most distinctive feature of European civilisation. (*ibid.*, p. 29)

While Childe's account now seems uncritical, he is at least grappling here with the particular problems of why the European cultural and economic development is distinctive, and from where it gets its particular cultural and economic 'style'. Even in the latest edition of *The Dawn* (1957) similar interests remain, and in *Man Makes Himself* (1936) there is a dialectical notion of progress. Development is cumulative and occurs through a continuous antagonism between progressive and conservative elements.

A more recent study (Lechtman 1984) demonstrates some of the same interests. Here the concern is to focus on the specific technological character of New World and Old World metallurgy, pointing, as Childe had done, to the elaboration of tools and weapons in Europe. Lechtman notes that the lack of a 'Bronze Age' and an 'Iron Age' in New World prehistory may have resulted from the importance of metals in warfare, transport and agriculture in Europe, whereas in the Andes, for example, metals had a more symbolic role in both secular and religious spheres of life.

Lechtman is thus interested in the specificity of a cultural sequence in the New World, and she is drawn to a particular set of cultural values which centre around the ritual and political significance of the colours gold and silver. Bronze was a late development in the Andes – other metals were used to produce the desired colours. However another set of cultural values prevented the Andean metallurgists from adding the gold and silver colours to the surface of metal items. A technically highly complex method was developed so that what was visible as colour on the outside of an object derived from the inside. 'The basis of Andean enrichment systems is the incorporation of the essential ingredient – the gold or the silver – into the very body of the object. The essence of the object, that which appears superficially to be true of it, must also be inside it' (*ibid.*, p. 30).

Lechtman supports this argument by reference to cloth production, which has the same 'structure' as the metal working (the design is incorporated into the cloth), and she shows the way in which the cultural values had ideological functions in legitimating domination within the Inca state. But the particular form of that ideology, and of the clothworking, and the particular technical process of electrochemical replacement and depletion, can only be understood in their own terms, related to practice but not reducible to it. Ultimately we will only be able to 'explain' the system of cultural values by going back in time, in an infinite regress.

Others (for example Coe 1978) have also been concerned to explore the particularity of New World culture as opposed to the Old World. Flannery and Marcus (1983) have argued, linking archaeological and linguistic studies, that Meso-American cultures over thousands of years have adapted to local conditions and undergone radical social change via a structured set of meanings, including the division of the world into four, colour-coded quarters and a 'spirit' termed *pe*. Although there is little attempt in their study to examine *how* structure, meaning and event are integrated, it is important that the ideational realm is shown in this example to have long-term influence. Furthermore, the ideational does not cause, or obstruct, or become reduced to the effect of, practical action; rather it is seen as the medium for action.

Within Old World archaeology, the vista has at times opened up, of working backwards over the long term to find the common cultural core from which European societies and cultures developed – this has been the concern of linguists and archaeologists involved with the Indo-European problem. But we can also incorporate a more detailed scale of analysis, trying to see how the different regions of Europe have been formed, divided and diffused. Christopher Hawkes, for example, has on a number of occasions noted the 'Western inhibition of furnished burial – or of burial altogether' (Hawkes 1972, p. 110) which leads to lack of status differentiation being expressed in indigenous burial customs in England (see also 1972, p. 113; 1976, p. 4). Such attitudes, or at least descriptions of behaviour, in relation to burial, are seen as continuing over the long term, and yet Hawkes allows for cumulative change, as in his discussion of 'cumulative Celticity' (1976) in which the Celtic style is traced back to its origins in the Bronze Age. It was in 1954 that Hawkes suggested a regional approach in which archaeologists used an historical method of working backwards through cultural sequences to find 'things common to all men as a species, inherent in their culture-capacity from the start' (1954, p. 167). 'It works as one peels onions; and so it reaches the final question, has the onion in fact got a central nucleus at all or is it just all peel?' (*ibid.*, p. 168).

Few archaeologists have attempted to use the great advantage of their data – that it covers long time spans – to contribute to such questions. Detailed historical studies of regional sequences which involve interpretation of subjective meaning are few and far between. We have already discussed (p. 28) the interesting work of Flannery and Marcus (1976; 1983), while Isbell (1976) has identified a 3000-year continuity in settlement structure in the South American Andes, despite major discontinuities in social and economic systems. Other important work of this type includes W. Davis' (1982) account of the principles or 'canon' of art identifiable throughout Egyptian history, Hall's (1977) identification of principles of meaning lying behind Hopewellian processes of economic and political change and interaction, Lathrap's (1977) account of long-term and widespread continuities in north-eastern American burial practices. In Europe, many archaeologists are aware of remarkable patterns of continuity which link the distant past to the present, particularly in Scandinavia, but few have made such questions the focus of research.

Equally, diffusion is now little studied as a component of cultural development. With diffusion decried as descriptive, processual archaeologists placed the emphasis on local adaptive sequences. Yet within the framework of the questions being asked in this volume, diffusion does have explanatory power. It can help to explain the particular cultural matrix. Objects or styles derived from other groups are given meaning in their new context, but these new meanings may be based on, and may bring with them, meanings from the old. The new traits are selected and are placed within the existing system, changing it. The aim should be less to classify different types of diffusion (Clarke 1968), than to see, for example, stimulus diffusion as an active social process working on and within systems of meanings which develop over the long term (cf. Kehoe 1979).

There is a danger that archaeologists will be content with vague continuities in cultural ethics, falling back on the excuse of their fragmentary data without adequate consideration of how subjective meanings are actively involved in society and in social change, and how they come to be changed themselves. In the work of Weber, and more particularly Sahlins, to take two examples, we begin to see how archaeologists might include both structure and process in their interpretations of the past, and we at last find approaches, stretching from Collingwood to modern anthropology, that adequately consider culture as meaningfully constituted, the active individual, and the historical context. But there is a long way to go before we can claim that the richness of such an approach, particularly as it relates to the content of historical meanings in relation to social practice, has been adequately applied in archaeology. The major stumbling block would appear to be methodological.

If archaeologists are to give more attention to subjective meanings, the 'inside' of events, how are they to do it? How do we reconstruct *mana*, Celtic spirit, Protestant ethic, European inventiveness, attitudes to left and right, from archaeological evidence? The problem develops like this: if we deny materialism, we can no longer predict the 'ideas' from the material base. Thus cross-cultural, predictive forms of inference are ruled out. If each historical context is unique and particular, how can we interpret it?

Historical theory and method: Collingwood

We have seen that in archaeology cultural meanings have frequently been thought to be derivable from the material world by applying cross-cultural generalizations. Lineage-based societies need a particular form of ideology (p. 63), or competition over restricted resources leads to bounded cemeteries and an emphasis on the ancestors (Saxe 1970; Chapman 1981). We have seen that Childe was concerned to identify the role of subjective meanings in social change, but his links with Marxism often resulted in methodological statements which are inadequate. For example, the problem of inference is discussed in detail in his *Social Worlds of Knowledge* (1949). Here mental categories are seen as being directly linked to social and economic structures. Using cross-cultural analogies with 'recent simple societies practising the same sort of economy with a similar technical equipment' (p. 19), the 'world-view of a neolithic Englishman' (*ibid.*) can be approached.

There are those who will follow Childe in accepting that worlds of knowledge are 'conditioned by the whole of the society's culture and particularly its technology' (*ibid.*, p. 23). Depending on the degree of conditioning that is allowed, this approach is more comfortable than one which denies such determination or domination of the economic over the ideational. Yet even in its own terms the approach is hopelessly flawed, since we do not even know the economy, the material base, without interpreting cultural residues.

Collingwood rejected Marxism or any other 'theory of universal history' with passion, in the same way that he rejected notions of 'progress' (and would probably have rejected the current equivalent, 'complexity'), and the methods of the natural sciences. Like Boas (1940) and Kroeber (1963) in America, he reacted against the superficial arrangement of cultural evidence, wrenched out of its historical contexts, into abstract schemes, calling it 'pigeon-holing' (1946, p. 265).

Collingwood, Boas and Kroeber were alike influenced by late nineteenth-century philosophers such as Dilthey, who made categorical distinctions between the natural and human sciences. In the natural sciences, 'objective' events are classified, relationships are sought between the categories, and laws developed (Collingwood 1946, p. 228). The human sciences, including history, systematize by seeing the particular fact more and more fully in context, among other facts structurally related to it. While history is a science in a general sense, it is opposed to the natural sciences because it works by having insights about context, it involves looking at the 'inside' of events. To study history is to try to get at purpose and thought. In the human sciences it is inadequate simply to describe correlations between objects (Collingwood 1939, pp. 109–10).

The emphasis on archaeology as a form of history is widely found in the period up to the 1960s in America and Britain, and it is probably true to say that it remains the dominant

viewpoint in much of Europe. Taylor (1948), while drawing a
distinction between archaeology and history, emphasized in
his conjunctive approach the 'inside' of cultural units, the particular internal relationships and meanings. Archaeologists in
Britain, many of them influenced by Collingwood, often emphasized the historical dimension of archaeological inference
(Clark 1939; Daniel 1962; Hawkes 1954). Piggott (1959) suggested that archaeology is history except that the evidence is
not intentionally left or recorded as history; it is 'unconscious'.
For Hawkes (1942, p. 125) cultures have both an *ex*tension in
space and time, and *in*tention in the social and economic field.
All viewed culture as involving norms and purposes which
were historically produced, but which could change over time.

While overarching norms and rules of behaviour are often
stressed, there is also much lip-service paid to the individual as
an important component in social theory. Collingwood, in
particular, has a well-defined theory of social action. 'What is
miscalled an "event" is really an action, and expresses some
thought (intention, purpose) of its agent' (1939, pp. 127–8).
He does not see action as a response to a stimulus, or as the
mere effect of the agent's nature or disposition (*ibid.*, p. 102).
So, directly in line with the point of view preferred in this
volume, Collingwood says that action is neither behavioural
response, nor is it norm. Rather it is situation specific, the
'event' being played out and manipulated according to bounded
knowledge of the situation. Because situations of standardized
types arise, action appears to be rule-bound, but in fact in
many aspects of life there are no rigid unchanging rules. Each
specific situation is so context dependent, with different com-
binations of factors involved, that it would be impossible to
have a full rule-book of behaviour. Rather, it is a matter of
'improvising, as best you can, a method of handling the situation in which you find yourself' (*ibid.*, p. 105).

As a result of this emphasis on action rather than event, a
recursive relationship between theory and practice is produced. Culture is therefore a cause and an effect, a stimulus as
well as a residuum, it is creative as well as created. Since they
incorporate individual action and recursive change, some early

viewpoints, particularly the stance taken by Collingwood, are far less normative than the New Archaeology, structuralist archaeology, or Marxist archaeology! All the latter assume shared norms and deny the role of the individual and of individual perception. They also all define behaviour as being rule-bound.

All these earlier writers allowed for generalization, at least after the reconstruction of cultural sequences. Yet they varied in their belief in the objectivity of data and in the use of natural science methods. Most believed that the facts did exist in reality, that the data themselves were beyond reproach, and that if one stayed close to the data, reconstructions could be secure. Piggott (1959; 1965) and Willey (1984, p. 13) also thought one could apply general concepts from elsewhere in order to interpret particular sequences. At the same time Hawkes, Piggott and Willey suggested that each cultural sequence was in some sense unique. For Willey (*ibid.*) 'the archaeologist must be immersed in the culture-historical contexts pertinent to the problems at hand'. For Piggott (1965) every civilization should be evaluated on its own terms. There is what might appear to us to be a contradiction, in much earlier work, between the subjective uniqueness of historical sequences, and an empirical and generalizing method, rather like that described as natural science.

For Collingwood, as for Daniel (1962) and Taylor (1948), on the other hand, the data themselves are more problematic and the use of cross-cultural generalization in interpreting historical data is denied. Collingwood pointed out (1946, p. 243) that, properly speaking, the data do not exist because they are perceived or 'given' within a theory. Historical knowledge is not the passive 'reception' of facts – it is the discerning of the thought which is the inner side of the event (*ibid.*, p. 222). How then, asks the positivist-trained archaeologist, do we validate our hypotheses? Well, certainly not through the application of universal measuring devices, Middle Range Theory. These would be, in Collingwood's terms, superficial, descriptive universal theories. How then do we proceed to validate?

Well, one answer is to say that we don't. Collingwood and

many other early writers imagined no security, no robustness, no proof. There can only be continual debate and approximation, and this is the view embraced in this book. But such an answer would be altogether too glib. As Collingwood was at pains to demonstrate, we can be rigorous in our reconstructions of the past and we can derive criteria for judging between theories.

The procedure to be followed is first to immerse oneself in the contextual data, re-enacting past thought through your own knowledge. But, as emphasized by Bourdieu (see p. 73), this is a practical living through, not an abstract spectacle to be watched. 'Historical knowledge is the knowledge of what mind has done in the past, and at the same time it is the re-doing of this, the perpetration of past acts in the present' (Collingwood 1946, p. 218). The past is an experience to be lived through in the mind.

What does Collingwood mean by this? Much damage has been done to the archaeological acceptance of Collingwood's position by the way he expressed this point. Collingwood did not mean that we should simply sit and 'empathize with', or 'commune with', the past; rather he is, in my view, simply stating the point made throughout this book, that all statements about the past (ranging, as we have seen, from notions like 'this is a hunter–gatherer camp', to 'this tomb functioned to legitimate access to resources') involve making assumptions about meaning content in the past. In this sense we do, whether we like it or not, 'think ourselves into' the past, and Collingwood is simply pointing this out. But he goes on to say that we need to be aware that we are doing it, and that we need to do it critically.

The 'reliving' of the past is achieved by the method of question and answer. One cannot sit back and observe the data; they must be brought into action by asking questions – why should anyone want to erect a building like that, what was the purpose of the shape of this ditch, why is this wall made of turf and that of stone? And the question must not be vague ('let us see what there is here') but definite ('are these loose stones a ruined wall?').

The response to such questions is dependent on all the data available (see below), but also on historical imagination, something which is very much affected by our knowledge and understanding of the present. Collingwood rarely discusses analogy, but it is my reading of him that he would not have been averse to its use. Analogy with the present clearly is important in broadening and exciting the historical imagination. However, this does not mean that one's interpretation of the past is trapped within the present – for Collingwood, it is possible to have insight which leads to understanding of a cultural context different from one's own. The mind is able to imagine and criticize other subjectivities, the 'inside' of other historical events (1946, p. 297). Although each context is unique, in that it derives from a particular historical circumstance, we can have an identity or common feeling with it; each event, though unique, has a universality in that it possesses a significance which can be comprehended by all people at all times (*ibid.*, p. 303).

The insight is then supported or 'validated' in a number of ways. For those working on material from the same cultural context of which they are members, continuity between the past and present allows us to work back, peeling off Hawkes' onion skins (above, p. 88), to see how thoughts have been modified and transformed. Alternatively, Collingwood emphasizes *coherence*. Since, 'properly speaking', the data do not exist, all one can do is identify a reconstruction that makes sense, in terms of the archaeologist's picture of the world (*ibid.*, p. 243), and in terms of the internal coherence of the argument. This strategy allows 'other' subjectivities to be hypothesized and it alllows us to differentiate between the theories. But the coherence also concerns *correspondence* to the evidence. Although the evidence does not exist with any objectivity, it does nevertheless exist in the real world – it is tangible and it is there, like it or not. Whatever our perceptions or world view, we are constrained by the evidence, and brought up against its concreteness. It is for this reason that I would find it hard to entertain the hypothesis that 'iron-using arrived in Britain before the advent of farming', or 'formal burial did not begin in Britain until after the adoption of iron': too much special pleading would be needed to make the evidence fit such statements. So, even within our own subjective perspectives, we often find it difficult to make our coherent arguments correspond to the evidence. At some point too much special pleading is recognized and the theory becomes implausible.

Thus our reconstructions of historical meanings are based on arguments of coherence and correspondence in relation to the data as perceived. Archaeology uses accommodative arguments; it has no other viable options. Clearly no certainty can ever be achieved in this way, but as will be seen in the examples presented below, knowledge of the past can be accumulated through critical application of the method.

Many people have been offended by Collingwood's views or at least by his way of presenting them, although in the intellectual climate of post-positivist philosophy several of his arguments seem scarcely radical. Childe was thus wrong to claim (1949, p. 24) that it is impossible for historians to re-enact in their own minds the thoughts and motives of the agent, since Childe himself continually imputed purpose and ideas to past minds as a routine part of archaeological work. And he was wrong to claim that 'Collingwood tells me in effect to empty my mind of all ideas, categories, and values derived from my society in order to fill it with those of an extinct society' (*ibid.*). Rather Collingwood argued that, standing within our own society, we can come to an understanding of other societies which it is unreasonable to claim has no relationship whatsoever with the nature of those societies. He suggested that we could critically evaluate our own and another society in terms of each other.

This is not to claim that our reconstructions of the past are independent of our own social context, and this aspect of inference will be discussed further in chapter 8. Rather, we have reached the position so far, that within the subjectivity of the data, there are still mechanisms for distinguishing between alternative theories. There is enough concrete contextual information in the evidence to restrict what we can say of it; it is the process of historical imagination which draws the evidence together into a coherence. Historical science is about criticizing and increasing these insights. Otherwise the data are used fraudulently within cross-cultural generalizations which overlook the problematic relationship between subject and object.

Some examples

It may be useful to provide some examples, taken from Collingwood's own work and from other more recent studies, of self-conscious attempts at reconstructing past motives, purposes and meanings. All the attempts are characterized by an immersing in the contextual data, asking questions of it, and reaching plausible insights about unique circumstances.

Collingwood (Collingwood and Myres 1936, p. 140), from his thorough knowledge of Hadrian's Wall and the later Antonine Wall in the north of Britain, asks 'Why was the Antonine Wall so different from Hadrian's? Why were there no milecastles and turrets, and why were the forts along the wall smaller and much closer together than on the earlier wall?'

The forts indicate that a smaller force was placed on the Antonine Wall. The construction of the wall also indicates an effort to be economical, especially in comparison with Hadrian's Wall.

> The ditch that lies in front of the rampart is even larger than Hadrian's but the rampart itself, instead of stone, is made of turf in the western and central part, of clay in the eastern. Hadrian himself had laid it down that turfwork was very much easier to construct than masonry. And the measurements increase the contrast. The turf part of Hadrian's Wall is twenty feet wide at the base; the Antonine Wall is only fourteen, which implies that, if the height of the turfwork was the same in the two cases, the Antonine rampart required, for any given length, only two-thirds of the turf that would be required by Hadrian's. The forts, again, instead of being massively walled in stone, with monumental gateways, were surrounded for the most part

with turf or earthen ramparts whose timber gateways were commonly of the simplest design; where stone was used, the construction was simple and inexpensive. Even the official central buildings in the forts were not uniformly of stone, and the barracks were of the cheapest, wooden hutments which in some cases had thatched roofs.

From this evidence, Collingwood moves to an interpretation of purpose. 'Both in construction and in organization, then, the Antonine Wall bears the marks of a deliberate effort after cheapness, at the cost of a serious decrease in efficiency' (*ibid.*, p. 142). This hypothesis is further supported by showing that the wall is not well-sited strategically, and by contrasting the Antonine Wall with a new frontier-line built in Germany. 'These various features of the Antonine Wall, when considered together, seem less like a series of oversights than parts of a deliberate policy, based on the assumption that a powerful frontier-work on that line was not needed' (*ibid.*, p. 143).

Collingwood goes on in this study to suggest why a wall of this type might have been built in this place at this particular time, relating his argument to further evidence about the tribes and settlements in northern Britain. But for our purposes, enough has been described to show the way in which, by asking and trying to answer a series of questions in relation to detailed contextual information, a particular, one-off, interpretation of subjective intent can be provided which is plausible and which can be argued through in relation to the evidence.

Collingwood's reconstruction relies to some extent on written records about the nature of the Roman army, and so it may be useful to turn to a wholly prehistoric wall, that constructed around the early Iron Age settlement in Germany, the Heuneberg. Merriman (1986) has shown how this wall can be seen to have been built in order to gain prestige. In answer to the question, 'why was this wall built?', archaeologists have noted the use of mud-bricks equivalent in style to mud-bricks used in the Mediterranean. They also note that in the north European cultural context such walls do not exist historically, and that climatically the conditions are unsuitable. Other contextual information includes the exchange of prestige items between the Mediterranean and this part of Europe, the internal complexity of the Heuneberg centre and the associated rich burial tumuli. All in all, the insight that this particular wall was intended more for prestige, to provide local standing, than for defence, seems plausible.

In their analysis of the Zapotec Cosmos in Formative Oaxaca, Flannery and Marcus (1976) demonstrate that highly symbolic representations on pottery can be traced to naturalistic versions, and can thus be given meaning as fire serpents and werejaguars. Similarly, I have argued (1984a) that many of the Neolithic tombs of western Europe mean houses. The argument is supported by noting eight points of formal similarity between the long tombs and contemporary long houses in central Europe. The meaning of the tombs as houses is then set within an appropriate social context. In an analysis of Neolithic axe exchange in Britain (Hodder and Lane 1982), we argued that the axes had a subjective significance beyond their utilitarian value because they were the only artifact type depicted in tombs; they were often placed in ritual contexts, as were symbolic chalk replicas.

None of the above examples is in any way remarkable – they are simply routine archaeology – but that this is archaeology is important. In the above examples analogy with ethnographic data may have influenced the choice of questions, the historical imagination and the theories espoused, but in all cases the main aim has been to grasp the subjectivity of past contexts, and to understand the data themselves, in their own terms. It might be felt that there are more than a few methodological gaps here. What is the 'universality' which Collingwood refers to (above, p. 95), how *do* we get at the past without just imposing the present, and beyond the examples given how do we interpret meaning content? Such questions will be returned to in chapter 7. But Collingwood's work has taken the search forward a long way.

Conclusion

So archaeology needs to go back to go forward. In the course of this chapter it has been found necessary to return to the pre-New Archaeology, to recover culture-history and to recover a coherent philosophical approach. I suspect that if one were to carry out an analysis of references or citations covering the period 1950 to 1980, one would find a sharp break around 1965. The New Archaeology dubbed all previous archaeology normative, descriptive, speculative, inadequate – it was time to make a break and start anew. Both the culture-historical aims and the interpretative methods were decried.

Of course there was much uninspiring culture-history, and much bad archaeology. But the same was to be true of New Archaeology, and will be true of all future archaeology. By examining various 'new' approaches that have been tried in archaeology over the past 20 years, I have shown that their limitations derive precisely from the rejection of cultural meanings, the individual and history. By attempting to rewrite archaeology as a natural science, knowledge accumulated in previous years (except in some cases chronological schemes and basic data descriptions) was set up as a straw man and knocked down.

In attempting to pull archaeology back into line and to reintegrate old and new, many will feel that I have gone too far towards the contextual and speculative. A common reaction to claims that we must interpret subjective meanings in the past is to point to problems of validation, to inadequate, mute data. In fact, however, it can be argued that all cultural reconstruction depends on imputing subjective meanings to particular historical contexts. In this chapter appropriate procedures as outlined by Collingwood have been discussed.

Another objection commonly raised is that to say a wall was built because someone intended to build a wall is hardly getting us very far. Certainly if no more than this was being claimed we would have got little further in one direction than Flannery's (1973) Mickey Mouse Laws did in another. But to discuss purpose and intention as deriving from a particular culture-historical context, linked into a framework of social action, is not simply to describe the data in a new way; additional information is provided. The interpretation goes beyond the data – if it did not the problem of validation would hardly arise. In the two 'wall' examples provided, construction took place in order to minimize cost in terms of garrisons and labour, and in order to gain social prestige. Both these interpretations add to the data.

Rather than allowing historical archaeology to become a 'new' natural science (Rahtz 1981), there would be benefits in transposing many of the methods and assumptions of historical archaeology into prehistory. In this chapter we have seen that history of the 'inside' of events, considered over the long term, provides us with the potential for a fuller understanding of social change, of the relationships between structure, idea and practice, and of the role of the individual in society. The archaeological data, with its unique access to the long term, can contribute to many contemporary debates concerning society and social change. For example, how resistant are subjective 'ways of doing things' to major social and technical upheaval? What is the relationship between gradual and sudden social change? By asking questions such as these, we can allow the particularity of the archaeological data to put its own case.

In the chapter that follows, an ethnohistoric example of the role of material culture in social change within a specific historical context will be described. But it must be borne in mind that for the moment I have been skirting round a problem of considerable implications. Collingwood (1946, p. 315) reaches the conclusion that 'we study history . . . in order to attain self-knowledge'. Because we have admitted that part of our reconstruction of the past is dependent on our own world view, and because we have denied that there is any possibility of certainty in our interpretations of the past, then 'every new generation must rewrite history in its own way' (*ibid.*, p. 248) as new questions are asked, methods change, and historical knowledge is expanded or altered. The ultimate aim can only be self-knowledge. In projecting ourselves into the past, critically, we come to know ourselves better. This is the reason for the passion lying behind Collingwood's rejection of the application of natural science to the human past. Collingwood's work was 'a political struggle' (*ibid.*, p. 167). To discuss humanity in terms of general laws, is ultimately to deny people their freedom. The historical approach on the other hand, allows that people are free to think as they want: they are not bowed before universal theories which they cannot subvert. Since the past cannot be known with certainty, we do not have the right to impose our own universals on the data and to present them as truth. I shall return to this theme in chapter 8.

6 An ethnohistoric example: reconsideration of ethnoarchaeology and Middle Range Theory

In the light of the discussion so far in this book I wish to use an ethnohistoric example of material culture change in order to throw doubt upon aspects of two currently fashionable aspects of archaeology – ethnoarchaeology and Middle Range Theory.

Ethnoarchaeology (Gould 1980; Kramer 1979; Yellen 1977; Binford 1978) is characterized by the leading proponents, Gould and Binford, as using a 'materialist', 'archaeological' method – that is, using objective, outside, non-participant observation to record the relationships between statics and dynamics. Part of the aim has been to produce Middle Range Theory, which, as Raab and Goodyear (1984) have shown, has been closely linked to site formation processes.

For Binford (1977; 1983) archaeologists need to develop arguments of relevance about the relationships between material culture and society. He argues that there should be *independent* measuring devices, 'thermometers', which can be applied to 'read' the archaeological data. While the idea of Middle Range Theory in relation to physical processes (e.g. decay of C^{14}) is feasible, it is difficult to see how there can ever be universal laws of cultural process which are independent of one's higher-level cultural theories. Of course, within these high-level theories there is a great need for research on material culture, processes of deposition and the like – one can call this Middle Range research. What is quite different, and denied in this volume, is that the type of measuring device discussed by Binford and termed Middle Range Theory can exist independent of cultural context.

The arguments in this volume also militate against a 'materialist', 'archaeological' ethnoarchaeology. The concern has moved from the 'outside' to the 'inside' of events. To understand material culture adequately, in its meaning context, will involve long-term participation in the cultures studied. The aim can remain the same – to ask archaeological questions of ethnographic data, questions which may concern material culture and/or the structures and processes of change; however the methods must be decidedly different. A problem then emerges. What is the difference between such 'inside', participatory ethnoarchaeology on the one hand, and ethnography and social anthropology on the other? Worse, will not social anthropologists, trained in the techniques of interviewing, recording, sampling, learning languages, and trained in a wider literature relevant to contemporary societies, do it better? Should ethnoarchaeology not disappear, to be replaced by or integrated with the anthropology of material culture and social change?

Ethnoarchaeology has only appeared as a sub-discipline within the last 20 years. In many ways it is a stop-gap, caused by the lack of anthropological concern with issues central to archaeology. If the two disciplines, with history, manage to converge, or at least to communicate more productively, then ethnoarchaeology may indeed become a 'period piece', associated with the non-contextual, cross-cultural trends in the archaeological science of the sixties and seventies.

Certainly there are signs (Miller 1983) of an increasing anthropological interest in material culture. Certainly, also, there are real difficulties involved in the retraining of archaeologists to undertake adequate in-depth anthropology. On the other hand, awareness of the need for a fuller understanding of all the dimensions of material culture is increasing in archaeology, and present material culture is the only arena where this hunger for archaeological knowledge can be played out. It seems likely, then, that ethnoarchaeology, ideally with a more 'anthropological' methodology, will retain a role in the immediate future.

Ethnoarchaeology is thus battling to survive on several fronts. There is the need for longer, in-depth research (often causing practical and financial problems). There is the realization by some archaeologists and anthropologists that trained ethnographers would do it better. There is a desire (Miller 1983, p. 6) to reduce the asymmetric dependence of archaeology on anthropology which ethnoarchaeology embodies. There is the realization within anthropology that the problems of material culture and change are interesting. And finally there is the problem that trends in archaeology away from the cross-cultural and towards the historical and meaningful are bound to impair the relevance of much recent ethnoarchaeology.

Although the ethnographic present may release some of its control over the archaeological past, it remains likely that the archaeological past will come to have a greater relevance to the ethnographic present. In this way ethnoarchaeology may be revived, but with an entirely new meaning. As ethnographers become more aware of the need for history to assist in explaining the present, they turn to archaeology to provide that past in areas without long traditions of written records. 'Ethnoarchaeology' here becomes the study of archaeology in ethnographic contexts in order to throw light on the ethnographic present. In this way ethnoarchaeology will become aligned with ethnohistory, both in definition and in practice.

Whatever the long-term future of ethnoarchaeology, it is clear from the arguments so far presented in this volume that it should be linked more closely both to anthropological and to historical theory and method. Thus the debate about ethnoarchaeology is just one instance of the general debate about the nature of archaeology. I hope to develop these points further in the example that follows.

Back to Baringo

The study I wish to summarize (for further detail see Hodder 1986) resulted from renewed work in the Baringo district, Kenya. Earlier work, described in *Symbols in Action* (Hodder 1982a), had left me with a question regarding a particular artifact type used by the Ilchamus tribe (elsewhere referred to as Njemps). The Ilchamus were the only group in the area who decorated their calabashes, incising them with rectilinear designs. Why?

In answering this question, one approach I could have followed would have been to test out some general theory or law-like generalization. For example I could say that, in comparison with nearby tribes, the Ilchamus decoration relates to greater social complexity in this group, hence the need for more organized and more symbolic display. Or the decoration relates to greater social competition and stress in this group, because there is a need to mark access to resources more clearly (Hodder 1979). Or I could argue, following Wobst (1977) that as the size of the social group increases and more interaction is needed with socially intermediate people, material symboling and style increase.

To 'test' these theories I hardly need to go to the Ilchamus – I can just look up the ethnographies to get the degree of social complexity, the degree of social competition or stress, or the size of this group in relation to other groups without decoration. Correlating with the decoration, I can then see which of my hypotheses fits the data – all very easy.

What are the difficulties with this approach, which now appears to be widely accepted in archaeology and ethnoarchaeology? The main problem is: even within the terms of this cross-cultural, adaptive approach, how do I know that the decoration has got anything to do with social complexity, competition or information flow? I may get *correlations* with these things, but I have not examined whether the calabashes and the decoration are used in such a way as to make these correlations meaningful or significant.

There are many other reasons why the social complexity/ information exchange type of approach is totally inadequate. It denies the role of active individuals, of meaning, of history, but above all it involves skating across the surface of Ilchamus culture. At best this leads to bad science; at worst it involves what might be called intellectual colonialism – that we can impose on the Ilchamus our own Western concepts, explain *their* culture in *our* terms, without trying to understand them, to let *them* teach *us*.

So it is possible to return to my question; why do Ilchamus decorate calabashes? Rather than taking Gould and Binford's 'outside', 'materialist', 'non-participant' position, and applying/ testing cross-cultural laws, I decided to immerse myself in the contextual information. What do the calabashes do, what do they mean?

Looking at the contextual information, some things are immediately suggestive. Calabashes are the only Ilchamus container which is decorated – pots and bowls and buckets are not. But not all calabashes are decorated: it is only those used to contain and serve milk which are, and especially those used to feed children. Each child has its own, or several, calabashes. Also, the decorated calabashes are 'female' objects – they are made and decorated and cleaned by women, they are used by women to milk cows, are looked after by women in the huts, and they are carried by women.

So, in explaining the decoration we need to consider the relationships between calabashes, milk and women; and because of the particular decoration of young children's milk calabashes we have to consider women in reproduction.

We can begin with *milk*. This is an important subsistence resource linked to the central importance of cattle (and to a lesser extent goats) as the main measurement of wealth. For much of the year, it is women who milk cows, look after the milk and distribute it to children and men. Linked to the real subsistence importance of milk is its central symbolic importance: it is used in many ceremonies as a blessing, it is mixed with fat and spread over the land to make it rain, the religious leader or *laibon* reads the future by looking in a calabash full of milk, and so on.

Remembering that it is *children's* calabashes which are particularly decorated, the Ilchamus have numerous rituals and symbolic devices to protect young children. Why are children so important? All Ilchamus men say, and this is a definite and oft-repeated statement, that their central concern is to have many wives and so have many children, so that they can have and pass on many cattle. Cattle, unlike land, are seen as a self-increasing resource, and they are used in bride payments – so the wealthier clans with more cattle can buy in more wives, have more children, and increase their population size through reproduction. Now, it is the bigger clans who are best buffered against disease and drought; thus the bigger clans can build up more cattle per head of their population and be wealthier. In terms of livelihood and economic and social support it is better to be in a big clan. But also, the bigger, wealthier clans are more important politically, in that they tend to provide the tribal chief and to have more political influence.

Children are therefore important to the male aim of increasing clan size. But they are also directly important in increasing clan cattle wealth in a number of ways. First, children play a role in looking after cattle, tending them. Second, by giving out one's cattle to one's sons, the cattle can be spread in different parts of the country where they are safeguarded or protected against local diseases and can take advantage of the variability in grazing. So sons are important in a family's or clan's concern to increase clan cattle wealth, as each son builds up his own herd. Third, daughters are important since it is through marrying out daughters that cattle are obtained from other clans as bride payments.

Agriculture plays a secondary role in male social strategies. To achieve their central aims based on cattle and children, *older men are dependent on women* as reproducers of children and carers for children in the domestic context. Yet this contribution of women is in many contexts denied by older men. In Ilchamus society decisions are made by collective discussions amongst elder men, and status and respect are obtained through being able to speak well. The opinion of women is not normally asked for in the public, political sphere, and they are not supposed to speak on matters of significance. In many contexts they are not supposed to speak in front of men. If I asked male elders what the viewpoint of women might be on a particular point they would often answer 'it is not for women to have a say'.

We can begin to see why, in the Ilchamus context, women might decorate milk calabashes. Men say they like to see women decorate calabashes well – it shows that the wife cares, that she takes time over and cares about feeding milk to children, etc. It shows that a man has a 'good' wife if she decorates the calabashes: it shows that she has some pride in her domestic child-rearing activities, and this implies a certain

acquiescence to his own interests – to what he thinks is important. Women also frequently express similar views – a woman
who decorates calabashes well is a 'good mother' and will more
readily be given help and support by other women.

But, in view of Ilchamus women's severe mutedness, their
silence in the public male world, I began to wonder whether
there was not also another direction to the decoration. It
seemed strange that women only decorated calabashes. After
all, women also feed children out of pots and do other things
that involve caring for the domestic context. It seemed interesting that the only decoration in the home concerned
resources highly valued by men – that is, cattle milk and
children. Now, we have seen that the full contribution of
women to society is denied by men who control the dominant
mode of discourse – overt speech. Perhaps, in the decoration,
women were drawing attention to their importance in society
covertly. In overt speech, and perhaps in their own conscious
minds, women express the dominant male view of society, but
covertly, or rather in daily *practice*, the decoration defines and
emphasizes the reproductive importance of women in a society
in which reproduction (of children and of the cattle which produce milk) is the central pivot of male power.

I began to think there was something to this idea when I
noted the contradictory statements made by men about the
calabashes. On the one hand they said, 'yes, we like women to
decorate calabashes', but on the other hand they went to considerable lengths to deny the importance of the decoration. 'It
is up to women, it is not our concern, don't talk to us about
the calabashes – that is women's work.' In this way, in the
dominant discourse, the female role is belittled or made peripheral.

The threatening role of the decoration is also seen if we
examine the designs used on the calabashes – particularly the
zig-zags, double 'V's, and crosses. If we look at the other contexts in which these occur we find they are linked to sexuality,
liaisons with young unmarried men, and ceremonies to do
with reproduction and witchcraft. In all these instances, women
are outside the control of the elders. In their close association

with the ritual leader, in female circumcision, and in witchcraft, women develop their own areas of activity and meaning, in the absence of the elders. The women also paint the 'V' design on young unmarried *moran* warriors, their lovers prior to forced marriages with the elders. The women talk about all these links of the decoration with ritual, young men, witchcraft, with vivacity and interest. They clearly have a practical consciousness of the relationships even if the significance is not felt or expressed overtly. It seems likely that at some level the design motifs themselves, imported on to the calabashes, do emphasize milk and children as areas of practical female control, like the other areas of control (female circumcision etc.) where the designs are used.

I hope to support the argument further later by showing how the practical control of milk and children has had historical effects; but for the moment there is a danger in putting too much symbolic and social load on these calabashes. As I watched women informally scratching the designs, lazily adding in a dot here and a line there as they chatted about the next beer-drinking session, I could not help wondering, 'am I really right to put all this significance on to the decoration – does everything have to have a social meaning?'

Certainly the predominant, indeed the only answer given to my attempts to ask directly, 'why are you decorating that calabash?' was 'because it makes it beautiful'. Surely I needed to give some credence to this strong indigenous view. And I began to feel that perhaps there was no social cause, perhaps the calabashes were just decorated as part of an aesthetic.

Certainly the social reasons offered above – the idea of covert negotiation of female control and the idea of male desire for female domestic care – do not *in any way* explain the decoration. I have explained the *functions* of the decoration, but that does not explain the style, the decoration itself – its becoming. We can see this clearly if we start from the social functions. In order to achieve the functions, women do not have to decorate calabashes; there are other ways to show one cares in the domestic context (keeping huts and children clean, putting protective charms on children, keeping the fire alight and so on), and there are other ways to exert practical control over children and milk – indeed men are effectively excluded from these areas anyway. Why do other neighbouring societies, which have similar pastoral-based economies, and similar concerns with cattle and children, not decorate calabashes? There is no necessary relationship between the social adaptive functions and the cultural style.

So, after all this, I still had not explained why they decorated the calabashes. I decided then to concentrate on the one solid clue that the Ilchamus had themselves given me. They had said repeatedly, in answer to my question, 'why do you decorate calabashes?', 'to make them beautiful'. It seemed I could only understand this aesthetic by going back into the history of the Ilchamus, in order to see how this idea developed.

The following brief account of aspects of Ilchamus history over the last 200 years is based on archaeological excavation (Hivernel, personal communication to the author), historical, ethnohistorical data and oral accounts (see Hodder 1982; 1986). In the nineteenth century the Ilchamus did not live in their present dispersed individual homesteads. Rather they lived in huge, defended, densely packed villages. They had few cattle and the economy was based on intensive irrigation agriculture. What was the context of decoration here? Calabashes were undecorated, as were pots and other containers. The only real forum for decoration consisted of female body and young *moran* warriors, plus one elder. Importantly, the great ancestral figure of the villages, the greatest ritual leader of the Ilchamus, who lived early in the nineteenth century and is accredited with strong magical powers, was and is called '*the decorated one*'. He was distinguished from other, secular, male leaders by the decoration of his skin clothing. When the Ilchamus say that decoration makes things beautiful, they mean many things. Their meanings are influenced by the historical associations with 'the decorated one'. In particular, the decoration asserts sociability within Ilchamus life. A proverb says that a person without beads wants to be alone. To be decorated, in a certain way, is to be 'Ilchamus' – the people who 'came together' in the villages; but the beauty is enhanced by the 'excitement' of its associations with ritual leaders and with subordinate groups such as young men and women.

This historical account does not explain why women did not decorate calabashes in the nineteenth-century villages. In the villages male interests did *not* centre on increasing repro-duction – the main source of wealth lay in the irrigation agri-culture. Agriculture had always had a low cultural status amongst the Ilchamus. Labour became a scarce resource, and was brought in from surrounding tribes, but within the Ilchamus it was women, not men, who were given the daily, tedious, low-valued field labour. It was not possible for women to provide this continuous labour *and* have many children, and birth rates were carefully restricted. This was not an appro-priate context, then, for women to decorate milk containers used to feed children. Men had few cattle and few children. Their strategies depended on grain, stored, cooked and eaten in ceramic, wooden and basket containers. But, again his-torically, it is only cattle, not cereals, that have high value for the Ilchamus. I do not have the evidence to explain where this value-system centred on cattle derives from; that is an archae-ological and historical question which awaits further evidence. But as a result, in the Ilchamus villages there was little interest in decorating cereal product containers, and it would have had little social effect.

We could always go back infinitely through time in this way, looking for historical associations, explaining one state in terms of its antecedents. Indeed it is part of the approach that I wish to advance in this book that culture-history from 'the inside' *is* a necessary part of archaeological explanation. But for the moment, let us continue onwards, having set the scene in the nineteenth century.

Around 1900 the Ilchamus abandoned their villages, obtained cattle, gave up agriculture and adopted their present dispersed settlement pattern. There are many 'reasons' we can give for this. The rivers by the villages silted up, necessitating a move; the British arrived and stopped inter-tribal raiding, so allowing dispersal; the population of the villages was getting too large; Arab trade routes had moved away from the villages; and so on. But all these factors are not reasons for change – they are only conditions of change, since in all cases the Ilchamus *could* have stayed living in the same or other large villages.

That they dispersed is because of a set of intentions based on historically-derived taken-for-granteds. As already noted, the Ilchamus despise agricultural labour, and wealth is counted in terms of cattle. Decoration is beautiful, but so are cattle. The lives of Ilchamus men are centred wholly around cattle, and the dispersal allowed clan competition and size to increase through the reproduction of cattle.

After the dispersal women immediately started decorating calabashes. As a part of the dispersal process, men moved to the recent and contemporary situation already described, in which their main concern was to have many wives and children so that they could have many cattle. Birth rates increased dramatically. Women no longer worked in the fields. It seemed 'natural' in this context for women to begin decorating milk calabashes – items connected with an aspect of life that everyone valued positively and thought important for various reasons. The calabashes became decorated as part of existing cultural dispositions within a new context. The principles and aesthetic sense concerning decoration were extended from female and young male bodies to the new arena of child care and milk provision in order to make *them* beautiful. But the new decoration was also exciting and dangerous: almost cheekily, it created a practical female domain regarding an aspect of cattle resources.

All Ilchamus men and women accept that after the dispersal women gained a new power and independence. This involved, for example, older women being able to 'own' resources (like cattle). Also, a practice was instituted whereby a woman could call for her husband to be tried and heavily fined by her natal clan. Although still minimal, women's power in society increased. The making of milk and child care 'beautiful' in a distinctively female way, through the use of decoration historically linked with women, young men and power groups (ritual leaders) within society, was part of this process of extending female control.

We have now come to the traditional and current situation described earlier in this chapter. But recently further developments have been occurring amongst some Ilchamus. Over the last 10–20 years a new phenomenon has appeared – the decoration of inside hut interiors. Again, this is done by women, using the old zig-zag range of designs used on the bodies and calabashes, and it is only the Ilchamus who do this.

In this recent period, many families have become less concerned with having large numbers of children, and more concerned with education, and employment outside Baringo or in administrative jobs. Male employment outside the area results in male dependence on female labour for production in the home, during the long periods (sometimes years) of male absence. High status amongst the young centres around having a Western-looking square house, with Western objects inside, and a Western-dressed, educated, literate wife. The new complex of ideas emphasizes hygiene, and babies are fed not with decorated calabashes but with plastic bottles and teats. In any case, male strategies include not only reproduction in the domestic context but also paid labour. Nevertheless men are now utterly dependent on their wives' labour in the domestic context, that is working the fields, looking after the cattle and bringing up the children.

In such families reproduction is not the central focus, but young women do still decorate milk calabashes (although clearly not those replaced by bottles), and they also decorate the huts, making the *whole* domestic context beautiful. The whole hut, not just part of it, becomes female. The historical connections are maintained in the form of the decoration and in its production (by women). Again, this is a 'natural' extension of existing principles, but it has the practical effects of changing the social meaning of the decoration and of extending the female domain. Older women now teach younger women, even unmarried ones, to decorate the huts. For everyone, this is just beautiful, fun, appropriate because of the 'inside' historical meanings; but also, because of the historical connections, other meanings and practical effects occur. The specific cultural attitudes are not neutral: they act back and lead to specific social consequences.

Indeed, the position of some women in contemporary Ilchamus society is changing radically. While women still have little public, political influence, the new 'Westernized' women are involved in government sponsored 'women's groups', which run their own farms and machinery. I want now to use this process to provide a final example of the historical process I have been describing.

As noted earlier, the Ilchamus form the only cultural group in the region in which decorated artifacts (apart from simple beaded items) are made. Missions and government development projects have focussed on the Ilchamus calabashes as a potential item for sale to tourists, and have encouraged Ilchamus women to make them for sale, as a means of earning cash and starting local women's self-help farming projects. In most cases, Ilchamus men would control very carefully any direct links between the women and government agencies and the outside world, and also much of the cash that women might earn. But women *have* been able to respond to the outside demand for calabashes and make their own cash in this way. This is because, as we saw earlier, men reacted to the female control of milk calabashes by saying, 'that is a woman's concern'. Women say that decorated calabashes can be sold by them because 'men do not care about calabashes'. As a result women can make cash, start farming cooperatives, ultimately buy tractors, and deal directly with the outside world. Finally they have become more 'outside' than men. Indeed development projects based on women often prove more successful than those involving men. It is ironic then that the 'unintended' consequence of the historic cultural attitudes surrounding the associations of 'decoration' and 'beauty', so long part of a social system in which women were controlled within the domestic sphere, has been that many women have actually become more active participants in the outside world than many men.

Conclusion

I have used this example of historical change in Baringo to
show that by concentrating on the social and conceptual context of material culture production, rather than by too easily
imposing cross-cultural laws, a complex world is opened up. I
have tried to show that the social process is negotiated between different interest groups within their overlapping cultural assumptions. Here I have concentrated on women and
men rather than on other social divisions, such as that between young and old in Ilchamus society. Individuals in the
male–female interest groups, see the world through historically-
tinted glasses; they work and live through a set of historical
assumptions. These historical taken-for-granteds are not just
cultural rules – if they were, there would be no dynamism, no
cultural achievement, no good or bad style, no direction.
Rather, the cultural rules are inseparable from aesthetic senses
and emotional qualities of desire, pride and so on. In this way
the cultural assumptions, when activated in a social context,
provide the motivations both for social change (as in the dispersal from the villages), and for material culture production –
they have specific social effects. The assumptions or structuring
principles have no beginning and no end, but represent an
eternal human process. Transformations of these principles
may occur, through social actions, but always in terms of what
went before.

Getting back to Middle Range Theory, we see that there can
be no universal cultural relationship between statics and
dynamics, because the historically contextual structuring principles intervene. Thus the notion that Middle Range Theory is
distinctive because it involves independent theory which can
be used to test other theories is false. The cultural processes
which form the archaeological record are not independent of
our general understanding of culture and society. It can also
be claimed that Middle Range Theory is distinctive because it
falls between general, global theory and data: for example, discussion of the symbolic and cognitive dimensions of site formation processes might be termed middle range. But it is not

clear to me why such a discussion is less global than a discussion of, for example, the causes of social complexity or the relationships between meaning and action. Middle Range Theory may be middle range when applied to data. But all theory has both general and applied forms. Once again the term seems redundant.

Getting back to the methods of ethnoarchaeology, we see that these should involve study from the inside, participation, and historical analysis. We can never understand anything in its present moment – we must always refer to the past and to the process of becoming in the present. As ethnoarchaeology becomes more like anthropology and ethnohistory, and as it needs to incorporate the methods of these adjacent disciplines more fully, its independent existence comes under threat – at least in its present form. In its place we are likely to find material culture studies, sitting astride many disciplines, and a different ethnoarchaeology, concerned with the archaeology of ethnic groups and with an archaeological dimension to ethnohistory.

7 Contextual archaeology

Ilchamus calabashes thus cannot be explained adequately by reference to universal functions – their particular meanings must be understood. The same can be said for all items of material culture and for all human action. *Whatever* questions one asks about the human past, even if it is only about technology or economy, frameworks of meaning intervene. After all, one cannot say what the economy of a site was until one has made hypotheses or assumptions about the symbolic meaning of bone discard.

This book, then, has been an attempt to consider various approaches to this problem. The search has been for an adequate answer to the problem of how we infer past cultural meanings. Now it could be claimed, following a Kuhnian conception of science, that one cannot compare paradigms such as processual archaeology, structuralism and Marxism because each has its own rules, language and perspective of data. There is, according to this view, no objective way of comparing paradigms; each is consistent in its own terms, with its own frame of reference. While I would accept many aspects of the position put forward by Kuhn, I would argue that the different approaches *can* be compared, in the same way that I will argue that alien cultures can be understood and then compared.

The original task of comparing and contrasting the different approaches in terms of their contributions to the questions asked in chapter 1, has now been achieved, and much of what was sought has been found. New developments in Marxist-influenced archaeology and social theory have led to a full discussion of the role of the individual in society, and a parallel account is provided by Collingwood, for whom history also plays a full part in the explanation. The notion that culture is meaningfully constituted is contributed to by structuralist archaeology; but, again, it is only in historical studies that include some degree of idealism that the content of symbolic meanings is given an adequate role.

Collingwood, as was shown in chapter 5, also provides methodological guidelines for the reconstruction of meaning content, but it was noted (p. 99) that problems and gaps remain. Also, Collingwood's account of method remains rather abstract. How does the archaeologist actually get down to reconstructing symbolic meaning in the past? In answering this question, and in filling in and extending Collingwood's account, I wish to describe in greater detail what I have elsewhere called 'contextual archaeology' (Hodder 1982a).

The word 'context' is used frequently in archaeological discourse, in questions such as 'what is the context of your remark?', or 'what is the data context?' The word is used in a variety of different situations to mean sensitivity to the particular data: 'your general idea does not work in my context'.

'Context' comes from the Latin *contexere*, meaning to weave, join together, connect. In reaction to the excessive claims about general laws made by some New Archaeologists (e.g. Watson, Leblanc and Redman 1971) one can argue that there were many movements in the contextual direction. As already noted (p. 30), Flannery (1973) reacted against too strong an emphasis on 'law-and-order', and emphasized instead 'systemness' – a more flexible approach in which particular relationships could be taken into account. This interweaving, or connecting, of things in their historical particularity has been described above (p. 77) as evident in many branches of archaeology (Marxist, evolutionary, processual). Butzer (1982) too has identified a 'contextual' method in ecological approaches to the past, and in Classical archaeology a contextual approach has been clearly outlined in relation to Greek painted pottery (Berard and Durand 1984). A recent book entitled *Contexts for Prehistoric Exchange* (Ericson and Earle 1982) seeks to emphasize the contexts of production and consumption in which exchange occurs.

In spatial archaeology more generally, I have argued (Hodder 1985) that a new generation of analytical techniques seeks to be more sensitive to the archaeological data, and to be more heuristic. We shall see more of this below. A major arena in which archaeologists have emphasized the particularity of their data is the study of depositional processes. Schiffer (1976) made the important contribution of distinguishing the archaeological context from the systemic context, pointing to the dangers of an application of general theory and methods (e.g. Whallon 1974) which did not take this distinction into account.

In Renfrew's (1973a) *The Explanation of Culture Change*, Case (1973, p. 44) argued for a contextual archaeology 'which alone deserves to be considered a new archaeology', and which involved linking general theories more closely to the available data. This concern with context has perhaps increased recently, at all levels in archaeology. On the one hand Flannery (1982) appears critical of general and abstract philosophizing which strays too far from the hard data; on the other hand, the concern with context has become a major methodological issue in excavation procedures. Rather than using interpretative terms (like floor, house, pit, post-hole) at the initial stage of excavation and analysis, many data coding sheets now use less subjective words such as 'unit' or 'context'. It is felt that excavation should not involve over-subjective interpretations imposed at too early a stage, before all the data have been amassed.

In a sense, archaeology is defined by its concern with context. To be interested in artifacts without any contextual information is antiquarianism, and is perhaps found in certain types of art history or the art market. Digging objects up out of their context, as is done by some metal detector users, is the antithesis in relation to which archaeology forms its identity. To reaffirm the importance of context thus includes reaffirming the importance of archaeology as archaeology.

In sum, archaeologists use the term 'context' in a variety of ways which have in common the connecting or interweaving of things in a particular situation or group of situations. Such concerns have often come to the fore recently. However, in this chapter I wish to go beyond the general definition of context so far discussed and consider a more specific meaning. By way of introduction, it will be helpful to consider two broad ways in which material culture can be woven together so as to be meaningful.

Two types of meaning

Two main types of meaning studied by archaeologists (similar to the two models identified in Patrik 1985) are the structured system of functional inter-relationships, and the structured content of ideas and symbols. Thus, in seeking the first type of meaning, we can ask about the human and physical environment, the depositional processes, the organization of labour, the size of settlement, the exchanges of matter, energy and information. We give the object meaning by seeing how it functions in relation to these other factors and processes and in relation to economic and social structures. The great contribution of processual and Marxist archaeology has been made to these arena. We have seen (chapters 4 & 5) that more recently emphasis has also been placed under this heading on the active social processes whereby individuals manipulate artifacts for social ends. The sorts of factors that might help to explain an object functionally have been broadened and are better understood as a result of all the developments since the early 1960s.

It is not adequate to extend such studies to consider the ideational or symbolic functions of objects; rather, reference should be made to a second type of meaning – the content of ideas and symbols. This involves more than saying, 'this fibula functions to symbolize women' or 'this sword symbolizes men'. Rather, the question becomes, 'what is the view of womanhood represented in the link between female skeletons and fibulae in graves?' The aim is to search for Bourdieu's habitus, the *pe* described by Flannery and Marcus, and other structured and structuring ideas of the type discussed in chapter 5. Archaeologists need to make abstractions from the symbolic functions of the objects they excavate in order to identify the meaning content behind them, and this involves examining how the ideas denoted by material symbols themselves play a part in structuring society.

As already noted, archaeologists have long discussed ways of using their contextual data to build interpretations of functional inter-relationships. This is the domain of palaeo-economics, exchange theory, information theory, systems theory, optimal foraging theory, social action theory, and so on. All such theories can be faulted because of their inadequate consideration of the second type of meaning with which the first is necessarily linked. My main concern here, then, will be with the content of meaning in particular historical contexts, since this is the main lacuna in current archaeological theory identified in previous chapters. The same point is made by Davis (1984, p. 12), Wells (1984) and Hall (1977). Although there is much overlap with the consideration of functional meanings, my main interest will be the use of contextual relationships to get at past meaning content.

How is this to be done? First, there is a need to be self-critical in the imposition of meaning. Are the meanings we impose on the past particular to our own cultural and social background? This is a matter of considering our context, and I shall return to this in chapter 8.

Second, we can consider the archaeological record as a 'text' to be read. Here we can begin a discussion which will lead to the specific definition to be given to 'context' in this volume, but which is closely allied to the wider meanings which have been given to the term within archaeology as a whole.

Reading material culture texts

The notion that material culture is a text to be read has long been tacitly assumed in archaeology. Archaeologists frequently refer to their data as a record or as a language. The importance of such an analogy increases when the concern is to discover the meaning content of past behaviour.

But how are we to read such 'texts'? Clearly, if the past material culture language had no common features, words, grammar or structure with our contemporary verbal language, then any such reading would be difficult if not impossible, especially since the surviving text is partial and fragmentary in addition to being simply different. However, I wish to argue that there are some very simple rules underlying all languages – or at least underlying the ways in which *homo sapiens sapiens* at all times and in all places gives meaning to things.

Most archaeologists would of course claim that their data are mute. Certainly an object as an object, alone, is mute. But archaeology is not the study of isolated objects. Objects in their 'text' may not be totally mute if we can read the language (Berard and Durand 1984, p. 21). Of course all languages have to be interpreted, and so, in one sense, all utterances and material symbols are mute, but a material symbol in its 'text' is no more or less mute than any grunt or other sound used in speech. The artifacts do speak (or perhaps faintly whisper) to us – the problem comes in the interpretation.

In arguing for principles which will allow us to read past texts and to see how their meanings change in different 'environments', it is important to make a distinction between language and material culture. Even though written language may have the same basic principles as material culture language (Hall 1977, p. 500), a written language is always very difficult to decipher even when much of it survives. This is partly because it is very complex, designed to express complex ideas and thoughts, and has to be fairly precise and comprehensive. But there are no grammars and dictionaries of material culture language. Material culture symbols are often more ambiguous than their verbal counterparts, and what can be said with them is normally much simpler. Also the material symbols are durable, restricting flexibility. In many ways material culture is not a language at all – it is more clearly action and practice in the world. In so far as it is a language, it is a simple one when compared to spoken or written language. For these varied reasons, material culture texts are easier to decipher than those written documents for which we do not know the language. This is why archaeologists have had some success in 'reading' material culture, even though they have rarely been explicit about the 'grammar' which they are assuming.

I take Collingwood to conclude implicitly that a universal grammar exists when he suggests (1946, p. 303) that each unique event has a significance which can be comprehended by all people at all times. This is also what I understand by Bourdieu's (1977) account of how a child comes to understand the world around him/her through observing simple associations and contrasts, and it is what I understand from our common experience of gradually coming to know another person or another culture. As we grow up in our own or another culture, and as we meet and get to know people, we can never be certain that we have properly understood what is in their minds, what they mean by things. All we have to go on is their grunts and actions in the world as we see them. Gradually, as more of these physical events occur, we come to some approximation of this 'otherness'. However 'other' it seemed at first, an evaluated approximation to understanding is feasible.

The universal principles of meaning which I wish to suggest lie behind such experiences are only those followed routinely by all of us as social actors, and by archaeologists in interpreting the past. I simply want to make these procedures more explicit, particularly in relation to archaeology and the type of data with which archaeologists deal.

In what follows, the term 'contextual' will refer to the placing of items 'with their texts' – 'con-text'. The general notion here is that 'context' can refer to those parts of a written document which come immediately before and after a particular passage, so closely connected in meaning with it that its sense is not clear apart from them. Later in this chapter a still more specific definition of 'context' will be provided. For the moment, the aim is to outline ways in which archaeologists move from text to symbolic meaning content.

Similarities and differences

In beginning to systematize the methodology for interpreting past meaning content from material culture, it seems that archaeologists work by identifying various types of relevant similarities and differences, and that these are built up into various types of contextual associations. Abstractions are then made from contexts and associations and differences in order to arrive at meaning in terms of function and content (see Fig. 6).

We can start, then, with the idea of similarities and differences. In language this is simply the idea that when someone says 'black' we give that sound meaning because it sounds similar (though not identical) to other examples of the word 'black', and because it is different from other sounds like 'white' or 'back'. In archaeology it is the common idea that we put a pot in the category of 'A' pots because it looks like other pots in that category but looks different from the category of 'B' pots. In graves, we may find fibulae associated with women, and this similarity in spatial location and unit of deposition encourages us to think that fibulae 'mean' women, but only if the fibula is not found in male graves, which may be different in that brooches are found instead of fibulae. Other associations and contrasts of women, female activities and fibulae

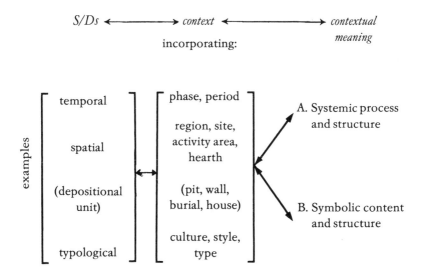

Fig. 6. The interpretation of contextual meanings from the similarities and differences between archaeological objects.

may allow an abstraction concerning the meaning content of 'womanhood'. For example the fibulae might have designs which are elsewhere found associated with a category of objects to do with reproduction rather than with productive tasks (see the Faris study, p. 62, and McGhee's analysis, p. 45).

We can formalize this process of searching for similarities and differences in the following diagram:

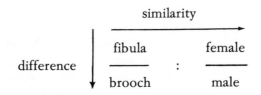

It is instructive to compare such a diagram with the following one, in which it is utilitarian functional relationships rather than symbolic functions that are being sought.

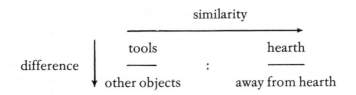

Here the archaeologist interprets the area around a hearth as an activity area because tools occur there in contrast to other parts of the site or house where tools are not found. The form of explanation is identical to the one above, in which the symbolic meaning of a fibula is sought. But, as has been claimed throughout this volume, there is no necessary disjunction between these two aims: function and symbolic meaning are not contradictory. Thus the fibula functions to keep clothes on and perhaps to symbolize women, and it can also have the meaning content of 'women as reproductive'. Equally the activity area around the hearth may indicate that certain tools have the meaning content of 'home', the 'domestic hearth' and so on. Indeed we need to assume some such meaning in order to look for the activity area around the hearth in the first place and in order to give the objects grouped there related functions. The identification of an 'activity area' is the imposition of meaning content. The two types of meaning (the functional, systemic and the ideational content) are necessarily interdependent – it is not possible to talk of the one without at least assuming the other.

The above account of meaning as being built up from simultaneous similarities and differences is influenced by the discussion in chapter 3, and it seeks to do no more than account for the way in which archaeologists work. However a prescriptive element is also present. First, it is argued that similarities and differences can be identified at many 'levels'. Thus similarities and differences may occur in terms of underlying dimensions of variation such as structural oppositions, notions of 'orderliness', 'naturalness' and so on. Theory is always involved in the definition of similarities and differences, but at 'deeper' levels the need for imaginative theory is particularly apparent. I will return to these different levels of similarity and difference below. Second, it can be argued that archaeologists have concentrated too much on similarities and too little on differences (Van der Leeuw, personal communication to the author). The whole cross-cultural approach has been based on identifying similarities and common causes. The tendency has been to explain, for example, pottery decoration by some universal symbolic function of all decoration or of all symbolism. Societies have been grouped into categories (states, hunter–gatherers etc.) and their common characteristics identified. Of course, any such work assumes differences as well, but the 'presence' of an absence is seldom made the focus of research. For example, we can ask why pots are decorated, but we can also ask why only pots are decorated. This is again partly a matter of identifying the particular framework within which action has meaning. If pots are the only type of container decorated in one cultural context this is of relevance in in-

terpreting the meaning of the decoration. But on the whole
archaeologists tend to remove the decorated pots from their
contexts and measure the similarities between pots.

The need to consider difference can be clarified, if in a somewhat extreme fashion, with the word 'pain'. One way to interpret the unknown meaning of this word would be to search for
similar words in other cultures. We would then form a category
of similar-looking words, including examples found in England
and France, and identify their common characteristics. But in
fact the word has entirely different meanings in England and
France, and one would quickly see this by concentrating on
the different associations of the word in the two cultures – in
England with agony and in France with bakers. This over-
simplistic example reinforces the point made by Collingwood,
that every term which archaeologists use has to be open to
criticism to see whether it might have different meanings in
different contexts. Archaeologists need, then, to be alive to
difference and absence; they must always ask questions such
as: is this pot type found in different situations, why are other
pot types not decorated, why are other containers not decorated, why is this type of tomb or this technique of production
absent from this area?

In what ways can archaeologists describe similarities and differences? In the fibula example given above, we already have a
typological difference (between the fibula and the brooch) and
a depositional similarity (the fibula occurs in graves with
women). We shall see that the interweaving and networking of
different types and levels of similarity and difference support
interpretation. For the moment, however, I wish to discuss
each type of dimension of similarity/difference separately.
Each type of similarity and difference can occur at more than
one level and scale.

The first type of similarity and difference with which archaeologists routinely deal is the *temporal*. Clearly if two objects are
close in time, that is, they are similar along the temporal dimension, then archaeologists would be more likely to place
them in the same context and give them related meanings. Of
course the temporal dimension is closely linked to other di-

mensions – if two objects are in the same temporal context but widely distant in space or in other dimensions, then the similar temporal context may be irrelevant. Diffusion is a process that takes place over time and space and also involves the typological dimension.

The concern along the temporal dimension is to isolate a period or phase in which, in some sense, inter-related events are occurring. So within a phase there is continuity of structure, and/or meaning content, and/or systemic processes etc. But what scale of temporal analysis is necessary for the understanding of any particular object? In chapter 5 examples were noted of continuities over millenia. It was also suggested (p. 88) that, ultimately, it is necessary to move backwards, 'peeling off the onion skins', until the very first cultural act is identified. This is not a practical or necessary solution in most instances; in most cases one simply wants to identify the historical context which has a direct bearing on the question at hand.

Archaeologists already have a battery of quantitative techniques for identifying continuities and breaks in temporal sequences (Doran and Hodson 1975), and such evidence is used in identifying the relevant context, but many breaks which appear substantial may in fact express continuities or transformations at the structural level, and they may involve diffusion and migration, implying that the relevant temporal context has to be pursued in other spatial contexts. In general, archaeologists have been successful in identifying the relevant systemic inter-relationships for the understanding of any one object (artifact, site or whatever). These are simply all the factors in the previous system state which impinge upon the new state. But in the imposition of meaning content, when the archaeologist wishes to evaluate the claims that two objects are likely to have the same meaning content because they are contemporary, or that the meanings are unlikely to have changed within the same phase, the question of scale becomes even more important. So, from considering temporal similarities and differences, we are left with the question: what is the scale on which the relevant temporal context is to be defined? This question of scale will reappear and will be dealt with later, but it seems to depend on the questions that are being asked and the attributes that are being measured.

Similarities and differences can also be noted along the *spatial* dimension. Here the archaeologists are concerned with identifying functional and symbolic meanings and structures from the arrangements of objects (and sites, etc.) over space. Normally analysis along this dimension assumes that the temporal dimension has been controlled. The concern is to derive meanings from objects because they have similar spatial relationships (e.g. clustered, regularly spaced). Again, a battery of techniques already exists for such analysis. It can be claimed that many of these spatial techniques involve imposing externally derived hypotheses without adequate consideration of context; however, new analytical procedures are now emerging which allow greater sensitivity to archaeological data. For example, Kintigh and Ammerman (1982) have described contextual, heuristic methods for the description of point distributions, and related techniques have been described for assessing the association between distributions (Hodder and Okell 1978), and for determining the boundaries of distributions (Carr 1984). Indeed, it is possible to define a whole new generation of spatial analytical techniques in archaeology, which are less concerned to impose methods and theories, pre-packaged, from other disciplines or from abstract probability theory, and are more concerned with the specific archaeological problem at hand (Hodder 1985).

In these various ways the archaeologist seeks to define the spatial context which is relevant to understanding of a particular object. In many cases this is fairly straightforward – the origins of the raw material can be sought, the spatial extent of the style can be mapped, the boundaries of the settlement cluster can be drawn. Often, however, the relevant scale of analysis will vary depending on the attribute selected (raw material, decorative style, shape). This is similar to the variation found if an individual is asked 'where do you come from?' The response (street, part of town, town, county, country, continent) will depend on contextual questions (who is being

talked to and where, and why the question is being asked).
Thus there is no 'right' scale of analysis.

This problem is particularly acute in the archaeological concern to define 'regions' of analysis. This is often done *a priori*,
based on environmental features (e.g. a valley system), but
whether such an imposed entity has any relevance to the questions being asked is not always clear. The 'region' will vary
depending on the attributes being discussed. Thus there can
be no one *a priori* scale of spatial context – the context varies
from the immediate environment to the whole world if some
relevant dimension of variation can be found linking objects
(sites, cultures or whatever) at these different scales. As was
made clear in the case of the temporal dimension, the definition of context will depend on identifying relevant dimensions of variation along which similarities and differences can
be measured, and this will be discussed further below.

It is perhaps helpful to identify a third type of similarity and
difference – the *depositional unit* – which is in fact a combination
of the first two. I mean here closed layers of soil, pits, graves,
ditches and the like, which are bounded in space and time. To
say that two objects may have associated meanings because
they come from the same pit is just as subjective as saying that
they have related meanings because they are linked spatially
and temporally, but there is also an additional component of
interpretation in that it is assumed that the boundaries of the
unit are themselves relevant for the identification of meaning.
Archaeologists routinely accept this premiss; indeed co-
occurrence in a pit, or on a house floor may be seen as more
important than unbounded spatial distance. Once again, similarities and differences in depositional unit can be claimed at
many scales (layer, post-hole, house, site) and the question of
identifying the relevant scale of context will have to be discussed.

The *typological* dimension also could be argued to be simply a
variant of the two primary dimensions. If two artifacts are said
to be similar typologically, this really means that they have
similar arrangements or forms in space. However it is helpful
to distinguish the notion of 'type', as is usual in archaeology,

since typological similarities of objects over space and time are different from the distances (over space and time) between them. Indeed, the notion of typological similarities and differences is central to the definition of temporal contexts (incorporating periods, phases) and spatial contexts (incorporating cultures, styles). Thus typology is central to the development of the contextual approach in archaeology. It is also the aspect which most securely links archaeology to its traditional concerns and methods.

At the basis of all archaeological work is the need to classify and categorize, and the debate as to whether these classifications are 'ours' or 'theirs', 'etic' or 'emic', is an old one. On the whole, however, this stage of analysis, the initial typology of settlements, artifacts or economies, is normally separated from the later analysis of social process. Most archaeologists recognize the subjectivity of their own typologies and have focussed on mathematical and computer techniques which aim to limit this subjectivity. After having 'done the best they can' with the initial, unavoidably difficult stage, archaeologists then move on to quantify and compare and to arrive at social process.

For example it may be claimed that there is more uniformity or diversity in one area or period than another, or that one region has sites in which 20% of potsherds have zig-zag designs while another adjacent region also has 20% zig-zag designs, indicating close contact, lack of competition, trade etc. But how can we be sure that the initial typology is valid? As in the example of the bird/deer drawing on p. 15, how can we be sure that the zig-zags, though looking the same, are not different?

To get at such questions, a start can be made with the structure of decoration (chapter 3). Do the zig-zags occur on the same parts of the same types of pot, or in the same structural position in relation to other decorations? But also, what is the culture-historical context of the use of zig-zag (and other) decoration in the two areas? Going back in time, can we see the zig-zags deriving from different origins and traditions? Have they had different associations and meanings?

In defining 'types', archaeologists need to examine the historical association of traits in order to attempt to enter into the subjective meanings they connote. To some degree, archaeologists have traditionally been sensitive to such considerations, at least implicitly. For example, through much of the Neolithic in north and west Europe, pots tend to have horizontally organized decoration near the rim, and vertical decoration lower down. Sometimes, as in some beaker shapes, this distinction is marked by a break in the outline of the pot between neck and body. In discussing and categorizing types of Neolithic pottery, this particular historical circumstance can be taken into account, with the upper and lower zones of decoration being treated differently.

Of course it can be argued that such differences, between upper horizontal and lower vertical decoration, are entirely imposed from the outside and would not have been recognized by Neolithic individuals. Certainly this possibility will always remain, but it is argued here that archaeologists have been successful, and can have further success, in recovering typologies which approximate indigenous perceptions (always remembering that such perceptions would have varied according to social contexts and strategy). Success in such endeavours depends on including as much information as is available on the historical contexts and associations of traits, styles and organizational design properties, as well as on a reconstruction of the active use of such traits in social strategies.

Thus, one contextual approach to typology is to obtain as much information as possible about the similarities and differences of individual attributes before the larger typologies are built. A rather different approach is to accept the arbitrariness of our own categories and to be more open to alternative possibilities. For example, the plant typologies used by palaeoethnobotanists tend to be restricted to the established species lists. It would be possible, however, to class plant remains according to height of plant, stickiness of leaves, period of flowering, and so on. These varied classifications can be tested for correlations with other variables, with the aim of letting the data contribute to the choice of appropriate typology. A similar procedure could be followed for bone, pottery or any other typology.

Four dimensions of variation (temporal, spatial, depositional and typological) have been briefly discussed, and one general point can be emphasized. An important aspect of contextual archaeology is that it allows for dimensions of variation which occur at 'deeper' levels than the direct comparison of forms. In other words, similarities and differences are also sought in terms of abstractions which draw together the observable data in ways which are not immediately apparent. For example, an abstract opposition between culture and nature may link together the degree to which settlements are 'defended' or bounded, and the relative proportions of wild and domesticated animals found in those settlements. Thus, where the culture/nature dichotomy is more marked, the boundaries around settlements (separating the domestic from the wild) may be more substantial, houses too may be more elaborate, and even pottery may be more decorated (as marking the 'domestication' of food products as they are brought in, prepared and consumed in the domestic world). The bones of wild animals, especially the still wild ancestors or equivalents of domesticated stock, may not occur in settlement sites. As the culture/nature dichotomy becomes less marked, or as its focus is changed, all the above 'similarities' may change together if the hypothesis that the culture/nature dichotomy is a relevant dimension of variation is correct. It is not immediately apparent that boundaries around settlements, pottery decoration and the proportions of wild and domesticated animal bones have anything to do with each other. The provision of a 'deep' abstraction suddenly makes sense of varied pieces of information as they change through time.

Relevant dimensions of variation

In any set of cultural data there are perhaps limitless similarities and differences that can be identified. For example, all pots in an area are similar in that they are made of clay, but different in that the detailed marks of decoration vary slightly or in that the distributions of temper particles are not identical. How do we pick out the relevant similarities and differences, and what is the relevant scale of analysis?

I wish to argue that the relevant dimensions of variation are identified heuristically in archaeology by finding those dimensions of variation (grouped into temporal, spatial, depositional and typological) which show significant patterns of similarity and difference. Significance itself is largely defined in terms of the number and quality of coincident similarities and differences in relation to a theory. An important safeguard in interpreting past meaning content is the ability to support hypotheses about meaningful dimensions of variation in a variety of different aspects of the data (see, for example, Deetz 1983, Hall 1983). For example, if the orientation of houses is symbolically important in comparing and contrasting houses (see above, p. 52) does the same dimension of variation occur also in the placing of tombs? There are numerous ways in which archaeologists routinely seek for significant correlations, associations and differences, but the inferred pattern increases in interest as more of the network coincides. Since the definition of such statistically significant patterning depends on one's theory, guidelines are needed for the types of significant similarities and differences that can be sought.

Here it is helpful to return to the distinction between systemic and symbolic meanings. As already noted, it is in the realm of systemic processes that most archaeological theory and method have been developed. Given such work, it is recognized that consideration of the sources of raw materials is significant and relevant to a discussion of the exchange of the items made from those raw materials. In discussing subsistence economies it is relevant and significant to study bones and seeds from a variety of functionally inter-related sites. But immediately, we are drawn in such accounts to the need to consider the symbolic meaning content of bones and seeds (see above p. 13), which has been less well researched and is less easy to define.

In discussing the content of symbolic meanings a start can be made with an example. Imagine we are concerned with the meaning of the occurrence of red pots on a site. What are the relevant dimensions of variation for determining the meaning of this attribute? With what should the red pots be compared in order to identify similarities and differences? A second, contemporary site has no red pots, but it does have bronze fibulae (which do not occur on the first site). Is the difference between the pots and the fibulae relevant for an understanding of the pots? Such a difference would be relevant if it were part of a more general difference in historical tradition between the two sites or regions, but since it is on its own we cannot say that the fibulae are relevant to the red pots unless there is some dimension along which we can measure the variation and see significant patterning. Thus, we might find that the red pots and fibulae occurred in the same spatial location within houses or graves – in such a case they would be alternative types when measured in terms of spatial location; or red pots on the first site might be contrasted with black pots on the second site, with the fibulae only found in the black pots. Once some dimension is found along which distinctive patterned similarities and differences occur, then the fibulae do become relevant to an understanding of the red pots. Our theories about the way material culture 'texts' work, including the notion of structural oppositions, allow statistical significance to be defined. In the case of the red pots, if no statistically significant patterning with the fibulae can be found, then we can describe in full the red pots without reference to the fibulae. In the example given on p. 126, the fibulae and the brooch are relevant to each other because they occur as alternative dress items.

As another hypothetical example, we can take the design in Fig. 7. If we want to compare this pottery design with other designs on pots in order to identify similarities and differences, we have to describe it in some way. But, *a priori*, there are very many ways of describing the same design, some of which are provided in the diagram. What is the relevant dimension of variation on which the designs can be described and

Design:

Descriptions:

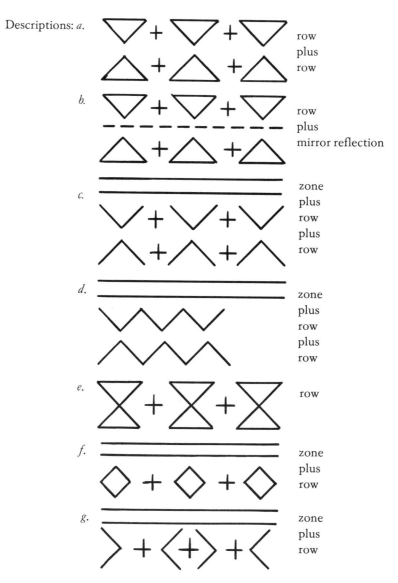

Fig. 7.

compared? It might be thought, and it is often claimed, that decisions by archaeologists about which is the 'right' description are entirely arbitrary. Yet we have already seen that much other information within the 'same' context can be used to aid the decision. For example, lozenge shapes (as in description '*f*' in Fig. 7) made of beaten gold might be found in the same graves as the decorated pots, apparently worn on male bodies as items of prestige. In fact lozenges might be found frequently in different but significant contexts within the same culture as the pots. This evidence for statistical association might lead the archaeologist to suggest that the '*f*' description in Fig. 7 was the 'best' in this particular context.

In this example we can continue further to define what is a relevant similarity or difference – along which dimension and at what scale. For example, at some point the lozenge used as comparison may be so distorted in shape that we doubt its relevance, or there may be such a gap in space or time between the lozenges being compared that we say that they are unlikely to have any relevance to each other; they have no common meaning. We can of course argue that the gold lozenges in graves are dress items, on a different depositional dimension to the pots, and therefore with different and unrelated meanings. Such an argument would have to demonstrate a lack of theoretically plausible dimensions on which significant patterning occurred in the similarities and differences between pots and graves.

It is, then, by looking for significant patterning along dimensions of variation that the relevant dimensions are defined. The symbolic meaning of the object is an abstraction from the totality of these cross-references. The meaning of an object is derived from the totality of its similarities and differences, associations and contrasts. None of these procedures can take place without simultaneous abstraction and theory. To note a pattern is simultaneously to give it meaning, as one describes dimensions of variance as being related to dress, colour, sex and so on. The aim is simply to place this subjectivity within a careful consideration of the data complex.

Definition of context

Each object exists in many relevant dimensions at once, and so, where the data exist, a rich network of associations and contrasts can be followed through in building up towards an interpretation of meaning. The totality of the relevant dimensions of variation around any one object can be identified as the context of that object.

The relevant context for an object 'x' to which we are trying to give meaning (of any type) is all those aspects of the data which have relationships with 'x' which are significantly patterned in the ways described above. A more precise definition for the context of an archaeological attribute is *the totality of the relevant environment*, where 'relevant' refers to a significant relationship to the object – that is, a relationship necessary for discerning the object's meaning. We have also seen that the context will depend on the types of questions being asked.

It should be clear from this definition of context that the boundaries around a group of similarities (such as a cultural unit) do not form the boundaries of the context, since the differences *between* cultural units may be relevant for an understanding of the meaning of objects *within* each cultural unit. Rather, the boundaries of the context only occur when a lack of significant similarities *and* differences occurs. It should also be made clear that the definition is object-centred and situation specific. The 'object' may be an attribute, artifact, type, culture or whatever, however – unlike the notions of a unitary culture or type – the context varies with the specifically located object and the dimensions of variation being considered, and with the questions being asked. 'Cultures', therefore, are components or aspects of contexts, but they do not define them.

In the interpretation of symbolic meanings, the significant dimensions of variation define structures of signification. One of the main and immediate impacts of the contextual approach is that it no longer becomes possible to study one arbitrarily defined aspect of the data on its own (Hall 1977). Over recent years research has come to be centred upon, for example, the settlement system, or the ceramics, or the lithics, or the seeds, from a site or region or even at a cross-cultural scale. Now, however, it is claimed that decorated pots can only be understood by comparison with other containers and/or with other items made of clay, and/or with other decorated items – all within the same context. In this example, 'containers', 'clay' or 'decoration' are the dimensions of variation along which similarities and differences are sought. Burial can only be understood through its contextual relationships to the contemporary settlements and non-burial rituals (Parker Pearson 1984a, b). Lithic variation can be examined as a structured food procuring process alongside bone and seed variation. The focus of research becomes the context, or rather the series of contexts involved in 'a culture' or 'a region'.

Within a context, items have symbolic meanings through their relationships and contrasts with other items within the same text. But if everything only has meaning in relation to everything else, how does one ever enter into the context? Where does one start? The problem is clearly present in the original definition of attributes. In order to describe a pot we need to make decisions about the relevant variables – should we measure shape, height, zonation or motif? The contextual answer is that one searches for other data along these dimensions of variation in order to identify the relevant dimensions which make up the context. Thus, in the example given above concerning lozenge decoration (p. 136), one searches along the dimension of 'motif' to identify similar motifs (as well as differences and absences – if the gold lozenges are only found in male graves we might be encouraged to think they are 'male' symbols when used on the pots, in contrast to 'female' symbols), and one finds the gold lozenge. But the lozenge on the pots and on the gold item of dress may mean different things because on one scale they occur in different contexts. One could only support the theory that the two sets of lozenges had similar meanings by finding other aspects of similarity between them (for example, other motifs used in male dress items which also occur as pot decoration). So everything depends on everything else, and the definition of attributes depends on the definition of context which depends on the definition of attributes!

There seems to be no easy answer to this problem, except that it is important to know *all* the data as thoroughly as possible, and gradually to accommodate theory to data by trial-and-error searching for relevant dimensions of variation, cross-checking with contextual information, and so on. The procedure certainly implies that interpretation of meaning will be more successful where the data are more richly networked. It was often implied, during the period of the New Archaeology, that archaeology would develop, not from the collection of more data, but from advances in theory. While such notions have their own historical context, the contextual approach is very much dependent on data. We have seen, throughout the descriptions above, that theory, interpretation and subjectivity are involved at every stage. Yet at the same time, the emphasis is placed on interpreting what the data can 'tell' us, and the more networked the data, the more there is to 'read'. As already noted, an object out of context is not readable; and a symbol painted on a cave wall when there are no deposits in the cave, when there are no deposits in the region that contain other depictions of the symbol on other objects, and when there are no graves containing the symbol, is scarcely more readable.

It is partly for this reason that historical archaeology is an 'easier' approach. Here the data are richly networked, much survives, and there are many leads that can be followed through, even in the absence of the literary texts, which themselves only provide another context in which to look for similarities and differences. The same problems remain – of having to define whether the written context is relevant to the other contexts (e.g. archaeological layers), and of deciding whether similarities between two contexts (written and non-written) imply the same or different meanings. Yet there is more possibility of facing these issues because the richer data allow more similarities and differences to be sought along more relevant dimensions of variation.

In prehistoric archaeology, the further one goes back in

time, so that survival rates diminish, the more difficult it becomes to ground hypotheses in data. Here the rare site with detailed information may often act as a key for numerous less well-excavated or poorly surviving sites. In many areas contextual archaeology can hardly begin until more data have been collected.

Explanation and description

Does all this mean that explaining the past is simply a matter of describing the contextual data in the fullest way possible? Much damage has been done in archaeology by the opposition of the words 'description' and 'explanation': 'descriptive' became little more than a pejorative term to throw at archaeologists who were not 'scientists'. It can be argued, however, that adequate explanation involves little more than a description in answer to a question. For example, consider the following sequence of questions and explanations:

1. Why was this site abandoned?   Because the population increased.
2. What is the relevance of population increase to site abandonment?   The site grew too large.
3. Too large for what?   The people had overused the environment.

In each case the explanation is simply a description of some events, although of course there is also an assumption that the response is in some way relevant to the question. So, in the response given in 3, it is assumed that people need to live off their local environment. These are the unexamined theories used within the explanation, but if we push and ask questions about these theories, we will again be faced by descriptions, either particular or general:

4. Why does it matter that they overuse their environment?

Because people live off the resources near them.

5. Why can they not use distant resources?

Because too much energy is expended.

It is always possible, therefore, to step in at some point along this chain of question and answer and ask another question, arguing that previous work has been too descriptive. Indeed, this has been the format of much of this volume, in comparing different approaches in archaeology. The alternatives offered may be more satisfactory in that they are broader and take into account important factors which had previously been neglected, and they may be more explanatory in that sense, but the explanations are only further descriptions. The example above concerns a settlement process, but the same can be said of interpretations of meanings and texts. The symbolic meaning given to an object is simply a description of aspects of its context and use. For example:

6. What is the meaning of this crown?

The person who wears it is king.

Thus, in many ways, explanation *is* description and description *is* explanation. In contextual archaeology it is necessary continually to ask questions in order to see whether the general assumptions are relevant in the particular context; this leads to full and detailed description of the total context as the whole network of associations and contrasts is followed through. This is a never ending process as new links are sought and old ones re-evaluated. The archaeologist plays on these data, bringing them to life as the composer combines the varied instruments of an orchestra in his score.

Contextual archaeology thus links adequate explanation to full description, as all the numerous influences impinging on any one trait or object are followed through. This is the point made by Case (1973) in introducing contextual archaeology. In history there is only a stream of continuous events, no

absolute hiatus, so the only explanation of change is a full
account of change.

It need hardly be said, given the discussion in this chapter,
that full description of contexts is not opposed to theory and
generalization. All description involves theories, meaning, subjectivity, generalization, and historical imagination. This is why
the archaeologist is more like the composer than the conduc-
tor of music. The ultimate aim of our detailed accounts may
well be generalization and universal laws, but initially, as scientists rather than as musicians or artists, our concern must be to
question whether the theories, generalizations and imaginative insights have the meaning we assume them to have in
past historical contexts. Contextual archaeology links question and data in a controlled way, governed by some general
principles about how we read texts, but even these general
principles must be open to critique.

A comment is needed here on the use of ethnographic analogy in archaeology. At one level ethnographic knowledge simply contributes to the historical imagination, inciting new
perspectives and alternative theories. But usually rather more
is meant by the term analogy: the past is interpreted in the
light of the present because of some similarity between them.
Information is transferred from the present to the past because
of observed similarities. This procedure is simply another instance of the general approach already outlined. In order to
use analogy one has to assess similarities and differences between contexts (Wylie 1985; Hodder 1982d). In comparing a
present society with one in the past, the procedures are similar
to those used in a comparison of two neighbouring sites or
cultures in the past. In both cases it is a matter of evaluating
similarities and differences between two contexts and discerning whether information can be transferred from one to the
other.

In both cases the main problem is to decide whether the
similarities and differences in the two contexts are relevant to
each other; thus archaeologists have greatest confidence in
direct historical analogies where the spatial context is constant
and the temporal gap is slight. Where cross-cultural analogies

are made, the problem becomes one of finding some relevant dimension of variation along which the similarities and differences can be examined, but over great distances and time periods, and when comparing societies in vastly different social and economic environments, it is difficult to know whether relevant relationships in the present were equally relevant in the past. For example, settlement size may be relevant to population size today, but it is not easy to say that it was so in the past. The use of analogy thus tends to depend on general theories which can provide arguments of relevance. It is the task of contextual archaeology to be critical of such general, cross-cultural theories, to examine more fully their contexts, present and past. Without the general theories there would be few questions asked of the past and fewer answers given. Without a contextual approach, the present and past become reduced to an assumed sameness.

Conclusion

In the discussion in this chapter an emphasis has been placed on methods of identifying and studying contexts in order to interpret meaning. It was noted that different types of meaning can be sought, varying from the structured processes of social and economic relationships to the structured contents of symbolic codes. When based on contextual analysis, these two main types of meaning can themselves be termed contextual.

The first type of contextual meaning refers to the environmental and behavioural context of action. Understanding of an object comes about through placing it in relation to the larger functioning whole. Processual and Marxist archaeology have tended to concentrate on the larger scales of this type of context, but the moment-by-moment context of situationally expedient action also needs to be incorporated.

Second, context can be taken to mean 'with-text', and so the word introduces an analogy between the contextual meanings of material culture traits and the meanings of words in a written language. The argument is that objects are only mute when they are out of their 'texts'; but in fact most archaeological objects are, almost by definition, situated in place and time and in relation to other archaeological objects. This network of relationships can be 'read', by careful analysis as outlined in this chapter, in order to reach an interpretation of meaning content. Of course, our readings may be incorrect, but misreading of the language does not imply that the objects must remain mute.

These two types of contextual meaning have a common characteristic also found in other uses of the term in archaeology (see pp. 119 to 120). All such uses refer to a concern with particular data rather than general theory. One of the aims of this volume is certainly to argue that general terms and theories must be better grounded in the particular context of study. Yet 'contextualism' does not equate with 'particularism', a term which has come to be associated in archaeology with the rejection of or lack of interest in general theory. Within contextual archaeology a recognition of the need for general theory and for theoretical archaeology remains, but rather, the concern is to demand a closer relationship between theory and data, placing one in terms of the other, and emphasizing inductive as well as deductive procedures.

Contextual archaeology involves the study of contextual data, using contextual methods of analysis, in order to arrive at two types of contextual meaning which are discussed in relation to general theory. But in discussing contextual archaeology it has frequently been found necessary throughout this volume to refer in passing to another type of context – the particular contexts of archaeologists themselves. This latter type of context seems intimately connected with the others, in a relationship which it is no longer possible to ignore. The context of the archaeologist is discussed in the next chapter, as part of a widespread series of changes in archaeology that can be termed post-processual.

8 Post-processual archaeology

Processual archaeology made contributions to archaeological theory by encouraging the notion of culture as adaptive, and by applying systems theory, information exchange theory and a host of other general theories. Many of these ideas had existed in some form in earlier approaches in archaeology, and the extent of this continuity will be further examined below. Yet perhaps the major contribution made by the New Archaeology was methodological (Meltzer 1979; Moore and Keene 1983, p. 4). Archaeologists became more concerned about problems of inference, sampling and research design. Quantitative and statistical techniques were used more frequently; procedures were questioned and made more explicit. Contextual archaeology is an attempt to develop archaeological methodology further.

In the realm of theory, there have been a number of developments since the early 1960s which, it can be argued, indicate movement from the initial stance of processual archaeology as represented by the early papers of Binford (1962; 1965) and Flannery (1967). The wider discussions and uses of Marxism and structuralism themselves express change. In this chapter I wish to summarize the main arguments in this volume in relation to the emerging characteristics of what might be termed a post-processual phase in archaeological theory. Three characteristics involve the breaking down of dichotomies, set up within archaeology, between individual and norm, structure and process, ideal and material. A fourth dichotomy, between subject and object, is also being pursued.

Norms and variability

Throughout this volume it has been noted that most current archaeological theory, of whatever hue, retains a normative

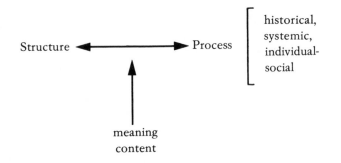

Fig. 8. The domain of post-processual archaeology.

component, in that explanation assumes ideas held in common and rules of behaviour. The only instances in which adequate accounts of individual variation and perception were encountered were those studies based on modern theories of social action and practice (chapter 4) and the work of Collingwood (chapter 5).

This finding is in direct opposition to the commonly stated aim of the New Archaeology to be concerned with variability. Certainly in some of Binford's recent work (cf. 1984) the notion of expedient, situational behaviour comes to the fore. As was noted in chapter 2, such interests have not made their way into archaeological consideration of ideology and symbolic meanings. Even in Binford's studies, individuals appear bound by universal rules concerned with what individuals will do 'if other things are equal'. Because Binford does not recount a meaning-laden process, the ability of individuals to create change and to create their culture as an active social process is minimized.

Norms and rules do exist. The argument here is rather that, in order to allow for change, innovation and the active individual, the relationships between norms, rules and individuals need to be examined more fully. In the practice of daily life, 'other things' never are 'equal'. It is always necessary to improvise expediently, yet through the framework of the norms and rules, changing them in the process. In this volume such questions have been discussed in the context of the relationships between the individual and society, and between practice and structure.

The first development that is found, then, in the post-processual phase, is the inclusion, under the heading 'process', of an adequate consideration of the ways in which individuals act within societies. For example, it is necessary to develop approaches to typology which are concerned less with defining 'types' and more with describing multi-dimensional surfaces of variability on which the 'type' can be seen to vary with context. More generally, archaeologists tend to force their material into styles, cultures, systems, structures, preferring to ignore the 'random' noise of individual variability. Leach's (1954) insight that various stages of development may be expressions of a common underlying structure is an important one for archaeologists who have tended to disregard variability: for example, there has been little account of how individual sites in a region may go through similar trajectories but at different, overlapping times (but see Frankenstein and Rowlands 1978).

The concern with variability is of particular importance in relation to social and cultural change. For example, it may prove to be the case in a particular area that most individual variability is allowed in areas outside the direct control of dominant groups. The decorated and varied calabashes described in chapter 6 provide an example of this. Social change may often result from, and grow out of, the ability to innovate in a peripheral domain, and again the Baringo calabashes provide an instance of such a transformation over time.

The recognition of variability in individual perceptions leads to a curious twist in the tale of the reconstruction of the content of historical meanings. In chapter 7 I discussed meaning content and how it can be attained in contextual archaeology, as if there is *a* meaning in the past. Ethnographers too often assume that there is some authoritative account of meaning that can be achieved. Certainly one has to allow for different perspectives from different interest groups in society (chapter 4), yet the problem goes far deeper than this. If material culture is a 'text', then a multiplicity of readings could have existed in the past. An example is the varied meanings given in British society to the use of safety pins by punks. It seemed to me (Hodder 1982d) that individuals would create verbal reasons for such items but that these verbal reasons were not 'correct' or 'incorrect' – they were all interpretations of a text in different verbal contexts, and in different social contexts. I had the same impression many times in Baringo. Individuals seemed to be making up the verbal meanings of things as I talked to them, contradicting and varying their responses as a social ploy.

As Drummond (1983) has suggested, the interpretation of meaning is not a matter of 'getting it right'. 'Do some people, because of privileged access to information, superior intelligence, perseverence, or whatever, *get it right*, come to know the meaning of the event, while others, less gifted or less industrious, only get part of the story and produce mistaken interpretations?' (*ibid.*, p. 193). Drummond argues that in practice the entity that we call 'culture' is really 'a series of questions and groping responses, and not a recipe-like set of answers' (*ibid.*, p. 171). The cultural reality is a shifting assortment of varied perspectives, so that, when looked at as a whole, there is no one 'true' version of events. The analyst's task is to identify these overlapping and often inconsistent versions and to understand their inter-relationships.

At first sight this notion of cultures as heterogeneous assemblages of overlapping, conflicting interpretations and representations of those interpretations, in an endless spiral of movement and variation, is disturbing to the archaeologist. Given the difficulty of interpreting *any* meaning in the past, how can the archaeologist ever approach this complexity of meaning? In fact, however, the potentials introduced by this insight are considerable. Archaeologists no longer need to force their data into well-bounded categories, and overlapping multiple dimensions of meaning can be sought using a contextual methodology. The *real* complexity of the archaeological data can be faced.

Perhaps more important is the link between variability of text interpretations and the discussion of power in chapter 4. The potential of individuals to 'see' things from different and contradictory perspectives may, in theory, be almost limitless. How, then, is meaning controlled by interest groups within society? Strategies might include placing events and their meanings in nature, making them 'natural', or placing them in the past, making them appear inevitable. More generally, material culture has a number of distinctive aspects which suggest that it may play a major role in the control of meaning variation. In particular, it is durable and it is concrete. All the dimensions of material culture elaboration discussed under the heading of 'contextual archaeology' – all the associations, contrasts, spatial and temporal rhythms and so on – can be used in attempts to 'fix' meanings. Much, if not all, material culture production can be described as a process in which different interest groups and individuals try to set up authoritative or established meanings in the face of the inherent ability of individuals to create their own, shifting, foot-loose schemes.

The 'fixing' of meanings may be most apparent at centres of control, and in public rituals. The various domains of culture, the opposing strands, may here be brought together, and the dominant structures re-established. A small contemporary example of the relationship between perspective and control may help to clarify the point. Walking in large, formal gardens one is often aware of some larger pattern. Glimpses are obtained of long lines of trees, shrubs, statues, lawns, ponds. In many parts of the garden one is not allowed to walk, and the individual understanding of the overall pattern remains partial and personal, dependent on the particular trajectory taken in the garden. Many of the formal gardens of which I am thinking are arranged around a large house, itself raised up or at the centre of radiating alignments. It is only from here, the centre of control, that the overall organization becomes apparent. Suddenly, from the centre, the scheme makes sense and the individual understandings can be placed within their context – a context constructed by the centre.

All aspects of cultural production, from the use of space, as in the above example, to the styles of pots and metal items, can be seen to play a part in the negotiation and 'fixing' of meaning by individuals and interest groups within society, whether child, mother, father, chief or commoner. Rather than assuming norms and systems, in the attempt to produce bounded entities, archaeologists can use their material to examine the continual process of interpretation and reinterpretation in relation to interest, itself an interpretation of events.

Thus post-processual archaeology, for the first time in archaeology, seeks to open up an adequate discussion of the processual relationship between individual and social norm. More distinctively, however, it does for the first time introduce something other than process.

Process and structure

Archaeologists have in the past been concerned with two main types of process, historical processes (such as diffusion, migration, convergence, divergence) and adaptive processes (population increase, resource utilization, social complexity, trade and so on). Although the work of Grahame Clark and Gordon Childe, for example, shows that both types of process have been studied for a long time in archaeology, it was the processual archaeology of the 1960s and 1970s that introduced a special emphasis on the latter form.

In essence, the two types of process are very similar. If a culture changes, we might say that this is because of the process of diffusion or because of the processes of population increase and environmental deterioration. Of course, as was discussed in the first part of this chapter, we can argue about whether diffusion is an adequate explanation, in the same way that we can argue about whether any processual account is adequate. Yet the manner of argument is always the same – visible event is related causally to visible event. It was on the inter-relationships, correlations and covariations between such events that a positivistic New Archaeology was able to build.

The notion that there might be structures, codes of presences and absences, that lie behind historical and adaptive processes, cannot exist comfortably with the empiricism and positivism that have dominated archaeology since its inception. In this sense, post-processual archaeology, insofar as it incorporates structuralism and Marxism, is a far more radical break than that which has occurred before.

There are dangers in talking of 'structure' as if a unified concept is widely accepted for this term. There are major differences between the types of social structure studied in Marxist archaeology, the formal and meaning structures studied in structuralist archaeology, and the technological structures described briefly at the beginning of chapter 4. Yet despite these fundamental differences, all such uses of the term imply something not visible at the surface – some organizational scheme or principle, not necessarily rigid or determining, that is immanent, visible only in its effects. Thus a new level of reality is proposed in archaeology, often described as 'deeper' than, 'behind' or 'beneath' the measurable evidence.

That archaeologists *are* able to discuss hypotheses about this different level of structured reality has been suggested by Wylie (1982) from a philosophical standpoint. In the account of structuralist archaeology in chapter 3, and of contextual archaeology in chapter 7, I have tried to outline some guidelines for a methodology for such analyses.

Historical meaning content: the ideal and the material

The third aspect of post-processual archaeology that can be identified is an increasing acceptance within archaeology of the need for, and possibility of, the rigorous reconstruction of subjective meanings. Within traditional archaeology the 'ladder of inference' (see p. 31) leading to the ideational realm could scarcely be scaled, and the New Archaeology often operated with the same attitude. For example, Binford (1965; 1982, p. 162) has claimed that archaeology is essentially materialist and poorly equipped to carry out 'palaeopsychology'.

We have seen throughout this book, however, an increasing readiness on the part of archaeologists to deal with the ideational sub-system, meaning structures and ideology. All such developments have played an important part in suggesting to archaeologists that systematic links can be identified between the material and the ideal.

We have also seen, in all realms of archaeology (p. 119), an increasing awareness that the particular historical context needs to be taken into account in applying general theories. The older law-and-order attitude has been faced with its own inability to deliver valid and interesting general laws.

Yet the ideational realm is, in most of archaeology, still studied largely in terms of the functions of symbols and rituals. And the historical context is no more, usually, than the specific conditions in phase *A* that affect phase *B*. In traditional archaeology too, meaning content was rarely examined; material symbols were seen as indicators of contact, cultural affiliation and diffusion. Only in chapter 5 were a few studies noted of an emerging explicit interest in meaning content as the 'cogwheel' for the inter-relationships between structure and process.

Insofar as post-processual archaeologists recognize that all archaeologists necessarily impose meaning content, and that such meanings form the core of archaeological analyses which must be made explicit and rigorous, the concern with meaning content is a third marked break with most recent and traditional archaeology.

Initially, the linking of meaning contents with historical particularism appears to have pernicious results for archaeology. A dangerous and negative pessimism lurks. How can archaeologists understand these particular other worlds, coherent only to themselves? In the discussion of contextual archaeology in chapter 7 and of Collingwood in chapter 5 I have attempted to demonstrate that increasingly plausible approximations to this 'otherness', in all its particularity, can be achieved. This is ultimately because historical meanings, however 'other' and coherent to themselves, are nevertheless real, producing real effects in the material world, and they are coherent, and thereby structured and systematic. In relation to the real, structured system of data, archaeologists critically evaluate their theories. The data are real but not objective;

and the theories are always open to further questions and new perspectives. There is no finishing position since there can never be any way of evaluating whether the 'right' interpretation has been arrived at (even discounting the different views of what was the 'right' interpretation within the past – see above p. 150). But better and better accommodations and new insights can be achieved in a continuing process of interpretation.

I have also argued (chapter 7) that the contextual approach should be distinguished from a rigid particularism in that general theory is acknowledged to be necessary to both the methods and aims of contextual archaeology. For example, a universal 'language' of material culture meanings has been accepted, which aids the 'reading' of past 'texts'. In addition, the aim of such 'readings' is to contribute to general understanding of the relationship between norm and variability, structure and process, ideal and material, and so on.

I have also argued that, despite the assumed universal characteristics of the material culture language, and of the way in which material culture is meaningfully constituted through similarities and differences, the perception of similarities and differences itself depends on creative insights which are partly subjective and historically dependent. We can continually seek better accommodation of theory and contextual data, yet that accommodation is evaluated as much on the basis of subjective experience (including analogical knowledge) as on any network of associations and contrasts in the data. Indeed, it is false to separate theory and data, since the latter can only be perceived in relation to the former. It is also doubtful whether theory can exist independent of data examples.

Such discussions open up a debate about the relationship between subject and object. And if every society and time can be expected to produce their own prehistory, what are the responsibilities of archaeologists to the worlds in which they live?

Archaeology and society: object and subject

Processual archaeology was not characterized by a detailed examination of the social contexts of archaeologists, since the main emphasis was to be placed on independent testing of theories against ethnographic and archaeological data. More recently, however, archaeologists have begun to show a greater interest in the subjectivity of the pasts we reconstruct in relation to contemporary power strategies. This development, a questioning of the separation of subject and object, theory and fact, is the fourth of the various strands of post-processual archaeology outlined in this chapter.

There are developments within theoretical archaeology itself which might be seen to have led to the new questioning of empiricist and positivist approaches. For example, the concern in post-processual archaeology with structure, if that term is used to refer to underlying or immanent organizational schemes, confronts any perception of archaeology as a discipline devoted only to observable, material remains.

The notion that meaning is contextual also appears to threaten established notions of universal correspondences between object classes (from 'tools' and 'sites' to 'hunter-gatherers' and 'states') and their meanings. As was discussed in chapter 2, attempts to place the new interest in mind and meaning within the tenor of the natural science, positivist model, have led to internally contradictory results.

As a result of the discussion of historical idealism in chapter 5, it was noted that Collingwood (1946) said that his intellectual life had been a political struggle. Although the archaeologist can be rigorous and scientific in the accommodation of theory and data, much of our definition of those data depends on ourselves. It is writers such as Childe and Collingwood who, from their Marxist and historical idealist positions respectively, discussed most fully the contemporary social basis of archaeological knowledge.

Thus, the post-processual interest in structure, mind and meaning, lead in theory to a greater concern with the present in the past. Although these new interests may provide an appropriate perspective and vocabulary for the emergence of a critical perspective in archaeology, it can be argued that some movement in this direction has resulted from recent increased confrontation of 'established' and 'alternative' archaeological perspectives. By 'established' I mean the archaeology written by Western, upper middle-class, and largely Anglo-Saxon males. The three 'alternative' perspectives I wish to identify as having an emergent impact on the largely non-critical establishment position, are indigenous archaeologies, feminist archaeology, and working-class and other perspectives within the contemporary West. In all these instances, two points can be made: first, the past is subjectively constructed in the present, and secondly, the subjective past is involved in power strategies today.

Indigenous archaeologies

Western archaeologists working in non-industrialized societies, particularly in the post-colonial era, became increasingly confronted both with the idea that the pasts they were reconstructing were 'Western' and with an articulate rejection of those pasts as being politically and ideologically motivated. The secure rocks of objective data began to seem more like shifting sands of subjective impressions. In many parts of the Middle East and of Africa, for example, Western archaeological interpretations have been rejected or reassessed and the Western archaeologists themselves excluded.

It can be suggested that the Australian government publicized anthropological and archaeological interpretations of Aborigines as 'natural', primitive and isolated. By processes such as these, the Australian Aborigines were denied another identity and their access to Western knowledge about disease, health, the law and power was restricted. On the other hand, Aborigines make use of archaeological interpretations in land claims, and similar strategies are used elsewhere, for example by the Canadian Inuit. In Europe, too, archaeology may legitimate claims about long-term residence in certain areas. For example, in Norway, debate about archaeologists' abilities to identify ethnic groups in prehistory is heightened by political issues concerned with Sami (Lapp) rights.

The United States of America, a country which has grown up through the relatively recent mass genocide of indigenous American peoples and which has even developed high positive values in relation to 'the frontier', has complex attitudes to the archaeology of the peoples it displaced. These attitudes have changed through time, but they have always portrayed America's native peoples as unprogressive (Trigger 1980). Thus in the nineteenth century native peoples were seen as unprogressive savages, a view resulting in the 'Mound Builder' myth according to which spectacular earthworks in North America were described as produced by non-Indians. In the early twentieth century, the same disrespect for Indians led to a lack of interest in explaining their cultural developments; a descriptive and static picture was painted. In processual archaeology, American Indians were treated as laboratories for the testing of general statements of interest to non-Indian archaeologists but of little relevance to the history or concerns of the Indians themselves (Trigger 1980). In all these ways, the Indians' place in America, and the Euro-American destruction of that place, are minimized, and archaeology contributes to an 'historical amnesia'. Recently, however, liberal tendencies and environmental resource concerns in Western society, coupled with Indian land claims and links between tourism and the cultural heritage, have led to Western archaeologists working on behalf of indigenous Indian groups in the United States and Canada.

The differences between Western and indigenous perceptions of non-Western pasts are often difficult to handle in practice. There is often considerable mistrust, misunderstanding and resentment. But it is difficulties such as these which have begun to push Western archaeologists to consider their own biasses and to confront the issue of whether differences in interpretation can be resolved by testing theories against objective data. In many cases the doctrines of verification are themselves perceived as political. The temptation is to withdraw

from the confrontation and the debate, rather than to expose
the apolitical nature of Western empiricism and positivism to
erosion.

Feminist archaeologies

It is this ability of Western archaeologists to note but ignore
the confrontation with indigenous archaeologies, which
emphasizes the potential importance of a feminist perspective
in archaeology. By 'feminist' I mean here a critical perspective
from the point of view of women in contemporary society.
Since this perspective in archaeology derives from a contemporary current within the West it is potentially less easy to
ignore than the archaeology of distant countries. This potential, while emergent (Conkey and Spector 1984), is far from
fully realized at present.

I do not intend to discuss the imbalance in the representation of women in the archaeological profession or the use of
sexist language in archaeological publications, although both
matters are linked to the main aspect of feminist archaeology
to be discussed here as relevant to the theme of this chapter.
Rather, I shall concentrate on two important points made by
feminist archaeologists (Conkey and Spector, *ibid.*). The first is
that archaeologists have tended to view the past sexual division of labour as similar to that of the present. For example,
hunting and trade are often seen as male pursuits, while gather-
ing and weaving are female. Projectile points and well-made
tools are linked to men, while non-wheel-made pots are linked
to women. This sex-linking of past activities makes present
sexual relations seem inevitable and legitimate.

Second, greater interest is shown in the 'dominant' male
activities. Males are generally portrayed as stronger, more
aggressive, more dominant, more active and more important
than women, who often appear as weak, passive and dependent. The past is written in terms of leadership, power,
warfare, the exchange of women, man the hunter, rights of
inheritance, control over resources, and so on.

These two androcentric strands of archaeological analysis
have been critically examined, in particular, in relation to the
debate about the 'origins of man' and 'man the hunter'
(Conkey and Spector *ibid.*), and reinterpretations of the 'origins
of man' have been made in which women play a more positive
role (e.g. Tanner 1981).

In relation to the two points made above, feminist archaeologists argue that, first, we cannot assume universally equivalent divisions of labour and sex-linking of activities. Rather
than assuming that the term 'woman' has universal cultural
characteristics, there is a need to examine the way in which
gender constructions can vary. Archaeological data are rife
with evidence of the cultural constructions of gender relations. Objects can be linked to women in graves, the
nutritional aspect of gender relations can be examined in comparing female and male skeletons, the representation and non-
representation of women in art and symbolism can be studied.
Indeed, it is often the absence of women from certain domains
of representation that will support insight into gender constructions. There is a need for contextual analysis, of the type
described in chapter 7, which places the biological category
'woman' in a social and cultural environment. The changing
'meaning' of women through time has been examined in a
contextual analysis by Gibbs (1986).

In relation to the second point made above, it is argued by
feminist archaeologists that women can play an active role in
society (see Tanner 1981). For example, pottery decoration
has been seen by archaeologists largely as a cultural indicator –
it is a passive indexing device. Even when viewed in terms of
information flow, exchange and interaction, the decoration
remains passive and unrelated to women. Feminist perspectives, however, suggest that in certain situations pottery decoration may be involved in the covert discourse of women who
are 'muted' in the dominant modes of discourse (Braithwaite
1982). Indeed, decoration and elaboration in the domestic
context may often have much more to do with the negotiation
of power between men and women than they have with symbolizing contact and interaction between local groups (see

Hodder 1984a for an application of this notion to European prehistory).

There is more than one type of feminist perspective: for example, debate centres on whether women in traditional societies do develop 'alternative models' of the world. Yet the overall impact is clear. Many of our most basic terms and taken-for-granteds are linked to contemporary perspectives and relations of dominance. One reaction would be to say that the past is therefore entirely relative – that woman and men must simply go their own ways with their non-comparable pasts. Yet it seems that another reaction is more frequently found – that the different perspectives can be argued through in relation to the data. Perhaps our own contexts and past contexts can be critically evaluated in terms of each other. This point will be referred to further below.

Other alternative Western archaeologies

From Creationists and readers of Von Daniken to metal detector users (Gregory 1983) and ley-line hunters (Williamson and Bellamy 1983), alternative and often extremely popular pasts are derived which establishment archaeologists may try to ignore, or dismiss as 'fringe'. Increasingly, however, direct confrontation occurs, particularly in Western societies in which the past as a resource has now to be used more effectively for the general public, as a commodity, well-packaged and responsive to demand.

In many Western countries archaeology has long been linked to the upper and middle classes. To what extent is this true today, how is the past used to legitimate established interests, and what are the effects on interpretations of the past? Recently a series of surveys of the British public's knowledge of and attitudes to archaeology has been carried out (Hodder, Parker Pearson, Peck and Stone 1985). Although these questionnaire surveys provide only provisional and initial indications, which need to be followed up by larger-scale and better constructed research, the main trends identified can be discussed.

From the surveys, it is clear that certain groups of people in contemporary Britain know more about the past than others. They have a broader and more accurate knowledge of what archaeologists write. They watch more archaeological documentaries on television, go more to museums and visit sites and churches, and read more about the past. Not surprisingly, these people have often had more education (stayed at school longer, or had some form of further education) than those with less archaeological knowledge. They also often have higher-valued jobs with more control over people and resources. The surveys also showed that such people are more likely to be male than female. Women tend to be less involved with archaeology and to be less knowledgeable about the past, wives often deferring to their husbands. Also, on average, younger people demonstrated greater archaeological knowledge than older people.

This pattern of archaeological knowledge in contemporary Britain can be correlated in various ways with the structure of work relations. For example, the amount and nature of leisure time available to different sections of society affects their ability to gain archaeological knowledge. There is some evidence that the working class, women in the home, and the elderly have relatively restricted leisure time, or else that their leisure is organized in such a way as to inhibit archaeological activities (Hodder, Parker Pearson, Peck and Stone, *ibid.*).

The pattern is in any case self-generating through the education process. Those who go to private or grammar schools are more likely to be introduced to archaeology than those who do not. While female archaeology undergraduates are as common as or more so than their male counterparts, by the time museum and university teaching posts are taken up, and books written, it is very largely men who become the curators, lecturers and authors. In these ways, male middle-class perceptions of the past are reproduced. The ideology of the dominant group is continued and controlled.

How exactly do these different groups in society interpret the past? The tentative survey results suggested that less educated, lower income groups tended to be relatively more interested in their local past, in archaeology as history, and in the immediacy of an experience of the past through archaeological artifacts. It is also possible to suggest general links between contemporary middle-class concerns and contemporary archaeological preoccupations. Relationships may exist between hyperdiffusionism and fascism, between archaeological hypotheses of environmental management and contemporary concerns with overpopulation and environmental depletion, and between recent archaeological uses of scientific positivism and current popular reliance on science to solve technical problems. Contextual archaeology undoubtedly has links with the 'anti-system' movements of the sixties, and contemporary emphases on meaning, the individual experience, and 'small is beautiful'. The varied viewpoints cannot all be divided on class lines. There is little evidence that ley-line hunters, for example, come from only one section of society. Rather, varied alternative pasts excite and involve many individuals and groups, in relation to the changing interpretations of establishment archaeologies.

Most individuals in the general public find it extremely difficult to develop their ideas about an alternative past in relation to the data from the past. They are excited by Von Daniken and films such as *One Million Years B.C.* and *Raiders of the Lost Ark*, and they develop their personal views about what the past must have been like, but they are kept at a distance from archaeological artifacts by glass cases, systems analyses and the jargon of social theory. Where they *do* manage to gain some access to an immediately experienced past, they are often directly confronted by the archaeological establishment, or else their views are studiously ignored. For example, metal detector users and the archaeological establishment in Britain have entered into a heated and acrimonious debate which serves only to widen social divisions (Hodder 1984b). Those archaeologists who do try to work with, rather than against, metal detector enthusiasts have found ways of encouraging cooperation and understanding (Gregory 1983). There is, then, great potential for archaeologists to encourage and help to create different views of and ways of participating in the past (Willey 1980). Attempts could be made to explain how the past is excavated (Leone 1983) and how it is reconstructed. Many museums, such as the Jorvik Viking Centre in York, are now more concerned with providing living versions of the past that can be experienced by the public. This is equally true of some well-established museums.

That there are dichotomies between the pasts produced by different interest groups, and that archaeology does not appear to have been successful in encouraging alternative perceptions and experiences of the past, may be linked to the role of archaeology and archaeologies in power strategies in Western society. A view of the relationships between knowledge and power which is currently being discussed in archaeology is provided by Critical Theory. This is of relevance to all critiques of establishment archaeology, including those deriving from indigenous and feminist viewpoints, but it is of particular relevance to archaeology as it is involved in class domination.

Critical Theory

'Critical Theory' is the umbrella term given to a diversity of European authors, particularly those of the 'Frankfurt school', centred around the Institute of Social Research established in Frankfurt in 1923 (Held 1980). The main figures are Horkheimer, Adorno and Marcuse. More recently Habermas and his associates have reformulated the notion of Critical Theory. The approaches followed in Critical Theory derive from the tradition of German idealist thought, and incorporate a Marxist perspective. Critical Theorists claim on the one hand that all knowledge is historically conditioned, but at the same time suggest that truth can be evaluated and criticism can be conducted independently of social interests – in short, that Critical Theory has a privileged position in relation to theory.

Among the various aspects of the work of Critical Theory that might be of most interest to archaeology, the analysis of aesthetics and contemporary culture is immediately relevant to the presentation of the archaeological past in museums, on television and so on. In their *Dialectic of the Enlightenment* Horkheimer and Adorno (1973) use the term 'culture industry'. Contrasting, for example, 'serious' and 'popular' music, they show that modern culture is standardized according to the rationalization of production and distribution techniques. Individuals do not 'live' art and culture any more – they consume its performance. The culture industry impedes the development of thinking, independent individuals; it conveys a message of adjustment, obedience. People are diverted, distracted and made passive. While there are many exceptions, archaeology in television documentaries and in museum displays is often presented as ordered, to be passively viewed. It is consumed as the cultural component of the leisure industry, rarely challenging and participatory. Archaeological scientists can place this sense of order and control and the supremacy of science (their own science and that of all dominant social groups) in a long-term historical perspective involving escape from the disordered primeval past through technological innovation. The result is a powerful ideological message.

Another relevant aspect of the work of Critical Theorists is their discussion of the philosophy of history. Habermas argues that it is inadequate to rest with the idealist interpretative understanding of contextual meanings, and the analyst must move towards the explanation of systematically distorted communication. In other words, one must see how the ideas of an age relate to domination and power. Similar points are made by Marcuse, Horkheimer and Adorno. In the *Dialectic of the Enlightenment*, the aim is to 'break the grip of all closed systems of thought; it is conceived as a contribution to the undermining of all beliefs that claim completeness and encourage an unreflected affirmation of society' (Held 1980, p. 150).

Following Hegel, the Enlightenment is seen as the rise of universal science in which the control of nature and human beings is the main aim. Within positivism, the world was seen as made up of material things which could be commanded and ordered according to universal laws, and the laws of history

were equated with the laws of nature. It can certainly be argued
(Hodder 1984b) that archaeological use of the natural science
model, positivism and systems theory supports an 'ideology of
control' whereby the 'apolitical' scientist is presented as essential for the control of society in past and future time and space.

In contrast, Critical Theory seeks a new enlightenment, an
emancipation in which critical reason leads to liberation from
all forces of domination and destruction. With writers such as
Lukacs, the insight which leads to this liberation is that the
structure of the social process constrains, dominates and determines the social totality, including thought and consciousness.

The ideals of objectivity and value-freedom are described by
critical theorists as being themselves value-laden. Critical
theory seeks to judge between competing accounts of reality
and to expose realms of ideology, and thus to emancipate
people from class domination. By emphasizing the material
and social conditions, ideological distortions can be revealed,
leading to self-awareness and emancipation.

A materialist approach to history as ideology has been taken
most clearly in archaeology by Leone (1982; see also Handsman 1980 and 1981). Leone notes that when the past is interpreted and made history it tends to become ideology, and he
suggests that the consciousness or revelation of that process
may help those who write or are told about the past to become
aware of the ideological notions that generate modern everyday life. Through, for example, locating the origins of individ-
ualism or modern notions of time in the growth of capitalism
in eighteenth-century America, visitors to museums could be
made aware of their own ideology as historically-based, and
their taken-for-granteds could be revealed as sources of domination.

While the notions of self-critique, and awareness of the
social and political value of what we write, are of prime importance in the further development of archaeology, the position
held by Critical Theory – as exemplified by Leone and Handsman – seems to me to be untenable for two main reasons.

First, such work embodies an unsatisfactory notion of domination. Society is represented as being ridden with all-

embracing, unified systems of representation. Leone (1982, p. 756) talks of imposing 'our own [ideology] in order to make ours appear inevitable'. As was discussed in chapter 4 in a critique of Marxist notions of ideology, there is no attempt to incorporate diversity in levels of awareness of social conditions. 'Society appears in their writings as steered from above rather than as the outcome, as I believe it to be, of a continuous process of struggle over rules and resources' (Held 1980, p. 365). However, there is evidence that different people in the contemporary public view the past in very different ways, and it is not at all clear that archaeology contributes to the maintenance of a universal Western ideology that prevents people from understanding their social conditions of existence. Indeed it seems that the past as constructed and experienced in contemporary life may reveal as much about the present as it masks.

The surveys referred to above suggested that individuals and subordinate groups in contemporary Britain are not easily duped by dominant interpretations of the past. Although dominated groups including the working class, women and the elderly appeared to have least scientific knowledge about the past, they scored highest in responses to questions about the need for the past. Individuals in such categories do think that the past and archaeology are necessary and worthwhile in giving meaning to the present. Yet individuals frequently showed a scepticism about the manipulation of the past by the media or by national governments; many people felt that little of what was said about the past by archaeologists and scientists could be proved in any way.

People are thus able to penetrate the aura of scientific knowledge that archaeologists attempt to present. They are bored by traditional museum displays; they turn off their televisions; they develop their own views of the past. A distinctive experience of those carrying out the public surveys was that, when asked about their views of the past or what it would have been like to live in the past, many people immediately began talking about the present, comparing and contrasting the two. Many talked of the advantages of contemporary technology and physical comforts, but felt that the world today was going too fast, that people had lost a sense of place in the world, that technology had gone too far, and so on. They had their own clear picture of what the past was like in relation to the present, and this picture was often different from the 'archaeological' version, providing an alternative to what people saw as good or bad in the world around them.

The second problem with current critical approaches in archaeology concerns the critique of those approaches themselves as historically generated. How can Critical Theory on the one hand claim that all knowledge is historical, distorted communication, and on the other hand be a critical means of enlightenment and emancipation? By what right or procedures does it accord itself a special theoretical status? The dilemma of critical theory in archaeology is: why should anyone accept a Marxist or critical analysis of our reconstructions of the past including the origins of capitalism? If the past is ideology, how can we presume to argue that only certain intellectuals can see through ideology to identify the social reality?

The special theoretical status which Leone claims in order to avoid the above dilemma is an avowedly 'materialist archaeology' (*ibid.*, p. 757). But if, for example, I do not accept the basic tenets of materialism, for reasons outlined in this book, I can claim that materialism is itself a false ideology – that it is just another universal theory developed by the academic community in order to maintain privileged control of the 'correct' interpretation of the past.

An alternative response to the second criticism made above is to argue that the past is not knowable with any integrity. The task of the archaeologist is, then, to choose any political stance he or she likes as a member of society, and to write the past so as to further that political viewpoint. This is certainly an honest reply which many may find attractive, but the potential results are disturbing. If the past has no integrity, and anyone's interpretation is as good as anyone else's, then archaeology is completely open to political manipulation by governments, elites, interest groups, and fascist dictatorships. With the data described as totally subjective, the archaeologist would have no recourse to the data in objecting to 'misuses' of the past. The past which was disseminated would depend entirely on power, and the ability to control theory, method and communication. In this volume, however, I have argued that the data from the past do have a contextual reality in relation to theory.

Conclusion

In the latter part of this chapter I have discussed the actual and potential archaeological viewpoints of a number of groups which can be described as subordinate on a global or intra-societal scale. These alternative, but by no means 'minority', viewpoints confront establishment perspectives and imply that the pasts we reconstruct are both subjective and involved in the negotiation of power.

It does not seem possible to react to this discussion of the contextuality of archaeological knowledge by claiming that 'method' will allow differentiation between the alternative interpretations of the past. Positivism, independent Middle Range Theories, materialist analysis, can all be seen to be tied to particular contemporary social assumptions; method too is ideological.

An open relativism appears at first to be the only solution, whereby 'anything goes'. Certainly there are some attractive aspects of this solution, if it allows greater debate between different viewpoints and a fuller involvement of archaeology in contemporary social and political issues. Yet most archaeologists feel that this solution is too extreme. Most feel that some interpretations of the past are not as good as others, that not everything can be said with equal integrity.

The contemporary social basis of our reconstructions of the past does not necessitate a lack of validity for those reconstructions. Our interpretations may be biassed, but they may still be 'right'. Clearly, however, it is important to understand where our ideas come from, and why we want to reconstruct the past in a particular way.

There is a dialectical relationship between past and present:
the past is interpreted in terms of the present, but the past can
also be used to criticize and challenge the present. In my view
it is possible critically to evaluate past and present contexts in
relation to each other, so as to achieve a better understanding
of both. There is a human mental ability to conceive of more
than one subjective context and critically to examine the
relationship between varied perspectives. This discussion
returns us to earlier statements in this volume about the
relationship between the larger whole (structure, system) and
the individual part (action, practice, the individual). Structures
and taken-for-granteds may well be the media for thought and
action, yet they can themselves be changed by critical thought
and action.

Thus the data are not objective but real. And there are no
universal instruments of measurement, but it is possible to
understand 'otherness'. Even the notions of the universality of
meaning construction must be subject to critical evaluation,
especially in periods prior to *homo sapiens sapiens*. We always
translate 'their' meanings into 'our' language, but our language
is flexible and rich enough to identify and perceive differences
in the way the same 'words' are used in different contexts. The
subjectivity of other objects can be comprehended without
imposing our own 'objective' subjectivities; the subject/object
division that has dominated archaeology can be broken down.

Post-processual archaeology, then, involves the breaking
down of established, taken-for-granted, dichotomies, and
opens up study of the relationships between norm and individual, process and structure, material and ideal, object and
subject. Unlike processual archaeology it does not espouse
one approach or argue that archaeology should develop an
agreed methodology. That is why post-processual archaeology
is simply 'post-'. It develops from a criticism of that which
went before, building on yet diverging from that path. It involves diversity and lack of consensus. It is characterized by
debate and uncertainty about fundamental issues that may
have been rarely questioned before in archaeology. It is more
an asking of questions than a provision of answers.

9 Conclusion: archaeology as archaeology

The term 'post-processual' attempts to capture a new openness to debate in archaeology – a broadening, to include the new dimensions under the four headings discussed in chapter 8, incorporating a variety of influences including Marxism, structuralism, idealism, feminist critiques and public archaeology. At the same time, the aim is to establish archaeology as a discipline able to contribute an independent voice to both intellectual and public debates. The contextual approach discussed in chapter 7 is one way of doing this which I personally find attractive, given my own views of the society in which I live and of what ought to happen to it, and given my opinion of the development of archaeology over the last 20 years.

In contributing to and being involved in broader interdisciplinary debate, archaeologists read various types of general meaning in their data. In Patrik's (1985) terms, I argue for two types of contextual meaning. One is the meaning of objects as physical, involved in exchanges of matter, energy and information; the concern here is with the object as a resource, functioning after its production, to facilitate organizational needs. The other is the meaning of objects in relation to the structured contents of historical traditions. In claiming that both views (object as object, and object as meaningfully constituted) are necessary in archaeology, I do not espouse a 'live and let live' policy in which both approaches can exist separately, side by side. There is little one can do by focussing only on the object as physical object. Perhaps distance from the source of an exchanged object, the amount of meat on bones, the efficacity of tools for cutting skin and so on, can be assessed without reference to historical meanings; but I have shown in numerous examples that most statements about the past involve making assumptions about such meanings – whether one is talking of prestige exchange, the economy or the population size of a settlement. Even words like 'wall', 'pit' and 'settlement' denote purpose. We cannot always assume that 'woman' and 'agriculture' mean the same thing in different contexts. Archaeologists have always worked by thinking themselves into past cultural contexts – one cannot get very far otherwise. The two approaches cannot exist separately because each is necessary to the other and is routinely involved in the other. The concern of this volume has been to argue for the necessity of this relationship, to argue that we should be more explicit and rigorous in our reconstructions of historical meanings, and that we should discuss the theoretical and methodological issues which result.

However, the reaction against such discussion in archaeology has been remarkably persistent. Much of Binford's writing today still centres on this theme. In an account of resin-processing activities amongst the Ayawara Australian Aborigines, Binford (1984) notes variation between Aboriginal groups. He asks whether this variation is expedient and situational or cultural, thus continuing the old split between process and norm, and framing the question on the assumption that such a split exists. Binford argues that variation in resin-processing depends on whether processing is carried out by mixed-sex groups using female-curated items, or whether it is done by all-male groups away from the residential camp. He concludes that resin-processing is situational and not culturally determined.

Clearly resin-processing may vary depending on whether women are present, and on where it is carried out. But to describe this variation and covariation is to do an adequate analysis of *neither* of Binford's two concerns – situational adaptation and culture. I have argued that situational decision making is a central part of context (p. 150); but to examine situational variability we need to have a clear idea of why women do certain tasks and men others, and we need to examine the active social context of male and female strategies in relation to each other. What are women or men trying to do in refusing to do this task in this residential camp, but not in that camp, and so on? Binford provides no answers to such questions. To examine the role of culture, we need to examine indigenous attitudes to the particular tools used in resin-processing, to those tools which can or cannot be used inside and outside the residential camp, to resin and resin-processing themselves, to men and women. We would need to examine such attitudes and strategies by observing more of the cultural context (what else do men and women do, what else are the different locations used for, and so on).

Rather than seeing culture and situational decision making as divorced, we can see them both as closely intertwined in each social 'action'. In Collingwood's terms, we need to get at the 'inside' of the Ayawara events. As in his Nunamiut study, Binford provides us with inadequate information to examine culture as the medium of action – the situational decisions, as described, occur in a cultural vacuum so that we cannot explain their specificity, their causes or their effects. The poverty of the argument is clear. Binford is more interested in making some general contribution to an abstract theoretical debate about which 'ism' is correct than he is in understanding the particular event in all its richness and complexity. The contemporary game of power is played out, but the cause of science is not necessarily advanced. Of course, we would return to the larger theoretical issues after having discussed Ayawara resin-processing in full, and general theories are necessary in the initial approach to and interpretation of the data, but in Binford's account the dialectical relationship between theory and data, the critical comparison of contexts, never takes place. Binford short-circuits the argument by 'testing' theories against pre-selected criteria, rather than trying to place the theories more fully in their contexts. Binford does not 'read' the Ayawara resin-processing 'text'. Discussion about 'isms' therefore becomes confrontational, based on *a priori* assumptions and on power. The contribution that the Ayawara could make to debate between the 'isms' is never realized.

In order for a broader, post-processual archaeology to be achieved, studies of the two types of meaning of material objects need to be incorporated. In this way the four general issues of post-processual archaeology (the relationships between norm and individual, process and structure, ideal and

material, subject and object) can be addressed. It might seem
that in becoming part of such debates, and using theories from
other disciplines, archaeology would lose some of its distinctiveness and independence. Post-processual archaeology is
part of wider concerns within social theory, and contextual
analysis derives much of its methods and theory from linguistic
analysis.

Yet it has also been argued in this book that contextual
archaeological data can be examined in their own terms, and
that the specificity of past meanings can be approached.
Perhaps archaeology can contribute its own data to the general
debates, using its own methods and theories to do so, as an
independent discipline. I wish now to examine the proposal,
again different from traditional and processual archaeology,
that archaeology is neither history nor anthropology, but just
archaeology.

The claim that 'archaeology is archaeology is archaeology'
was forcefully made by David Clarke. His *Analytical Archaeology*
(1968) is the most significant attempt to develop a peculiarly
archaeological methodology based on archaeological objects
and their associations and affinities in archaeological contexts.
In his later Glastonbury study (1972; see above, p. 50), Clarke
conducted a detailed contextual analysis incorporating a structural element. Apart from his non-alignment with the view
that 'archaeology is anthropology or it is nothing', Clarke dif-
fered from much processual or 'New' archaeology because he
retained a concern with cultural entities, their diffusion and
continuities. Despite a strong natural science element in his
work, he was suspicious of too easily imposing and 'testing'
general laws. There are clearly many similarities, therefore,
with the more limited account of a contextual approach provided in this volume. The major difference, apart from the
detailed type of methodology embraced, is in Clarke's failure
to identify ways of moving beyond the data to interpret them.
In *Analytical Archaeology* his scheme is analytical and empirical.
The social and cultural meanings of his archaeological patterns are far from clear. Simple cross-cultural interpretations
were imposed (for example regarding the significance of

regional cultural groupings), and there is little concern with meaning content and 'history from the inside' in this or any of his later works.

Taylor too had claimed (1948) that 'archaeology is neither history nor anthropology' (*ibid.*, p. 44). Again there are many similarities between the view put forward in this volume and his conjunctive approach, which had as its primary goal 'the elucidation of cultural conjunctives, the associations and relationships, the "affinities", *within* the manifestation under investigation' (*ibid.*, pp. 95–6). The aim was to examine contextual information in each unit or site as a discrete entity within its own cultural expression, with an emphasis on the cultural context in contrast to the comparative method. Further, 'culture is a mental phenomenon, consisting of the content of minds, not of material objects or observable behaviour' (*ibid.*, p. 98). In applied examples, Taylor demonstrates the ability of archaeologists to reconstruct ideas in the covert culture of past societies. For example, in an examination of cloth decoration Taylor notes whether cords are twisted to the left or right, and goes on to identify structuring principles, one being that Coahuila textile shows 'unconcern with regularized decorative wholes' (*ibid.*, p. 182).

Despite these clear similarities with the viewpoints discussed in chapter 7, there are some important limitations in his approach, recalling the critical comments made earlier in this volume. First, Taylor claims a categoric distinction between idea and practice: 'Culture itself consists of ideas, not processes' (*ibid.*, p. 110). This is the opposite to Binford's claim, and it is equally inadequate.

Second, Taylor's view is normative, although not in the sense that 'societies' somehow share an outlook on the world. Taylor suggested that culture can be either shared or individual and idiosyncratic. However, I would take issue with Taylor in regard to the second meaning of normative – that behaviour is rule-bound. Individuals or groups are so controlled by systems or codes or structures that they cannot usurp them. Taylor appears to talk of culture as made up of rules of this kind, rather than of contextual decisions informed by rules and dispositions. In this sense his approach is not contextual (situationally contextual) but normative.

Despite these and other differences with Taylor's approach (in particular Taylor does not develop a socially self-conscious and critical stance in relation to the subjectivity of data description and interpretation), it is clear that Taylor, in common with Collingwood, has much to offer contemporary archaeologists. It is not my concern to deny links to earlier archaeologists – indeed it seems necessary to rebuild the bridges which were so harshly broken by processual archaeology, and to re-evaluate what has been termed the 'long sleep of archaeological theory' (Renfrew 1983b).

In this volume, the notion that archaeology should have an independent existence, despite its involvements in general theory and method, has the following components. First, I have already commented in chapter 8 that archaeology can be distinguished from antiquarianism by its concern with the contexts of material objects. It has been argued that archaeologists can incorporate inductive methods in building up from contextual associations and contrasts towards a critical understanding of specific historical meanings. These readings and interpretations are translations in a different time; they make universal assumptions, but the results are not wholly dependent on the present. The readings inform and contribute to the present through critical evaluation of the past. How much archaeologists can interpret depends on the richness of their data networks and on their knowledge and abilities, yet there is a clear potential for independent archaeological contribution.

Second, while archaeologists may read material culture texts in ways comparable to the reading of historical texts, there are distinct differences between material culture and spoken or written language, differences which need to be researched further. Material culture often appears to be a simpler but more ambiguous language, and, in comparison to speech, it often seems more fixed and durable. In addition, most words are arbitrary signifiers of the concepts signified: thus, the relationship between the word 'tree', as opposed to 'arbre' or 'tarm', and the concept 'tree' is conventional, and historical.

But a material culture 'word', such as a photograph or sculpture of a human being, is not an arbitrary representation of that which is signified: thus, in contrast to the majority of words, many material culture signs are iconic. These and other differences imply that archaeologists have to develop their own theory and method for reading their own particular data.

Third, archaeology can avail itself of evidence of human cultural activity that covers enormous spans of time. This long-term perspective has the potential for leading to new insights into the four main issues in post-processual archaeology. For example, over the long term, what role is played by the individual event in the general processes of social and cultural change, and what is the relationship between structure and process? In the short term, it may appear that social and economic determinants are more important, but over the long term the social and economic decisions may be seen to form repeated patterns that have an underlying structural or cultural rhythm. Initial archaeological work in this direction was discussed in chapter 5.

In these various ways, archaeology can be seen as an independent discipline groping towards independent method and theory, but necessarily linked to and contributing to general social theory. The problem of the relationship between the particular and the general which underlies the three points discussed in the previous paragraphs, is itself a wide issue to which archaeology can make a particular contribution.

Archaeological objects raise questions about the relationship between the specific and the general, in an extreme and evocative form. This relationship, apparently ignored in much recent academic archaeology, has been captured by Mags Harries in her public art on the streets of Boston (frontispiece). Her art is claimed as archaeological, first because she recognizes the close immediacy of everyday mundane objects, their historical specificity. Often produced to be left behind, unintended and unnoticed, the objects capture a fleeting moment in concrete form. Second, however, we feel that we understand the objects, that there is a commonality and nearness, even over great expanses of time. We are confronted by the enormity of time and the generality of experience. In this volume I have tried to argue that we can understand this distance and generality only by exploiting to the full the concrete everydayness of the artifacts themselves, in all their specificity.

On the streets of Boston, Mags Harries creates archaeological objects. Her art is archaeological in the two senses just defined. For archaeology itself to become archaeological once again, will involve more than digging up more artifacts and putting them in museums and into socio-cultural sub-systems – we need to examine the specific contexts of objects in the past, in order to debate our own contexts in the face of the generality of the long term.

In discussing tentative steps in these directions, this volume intentionally raises more questions than it answers – about the relationships between individuals and societies, about the existence of general laws, about the role of archaeologists in society, and so on. The meaning of the past is more complex than we might have thought. However, rather than taking the line that archaeology now appears hopelessly difficult, I have in fact suggested that archaeologists can return to basic principles in translating the meaning of past texts into their own contemporary language. The methods of excavation and interpretation based on the notion of context are well-developed. Using such methods – Collingwood's question-and-answer procedure, notions of coherence and correspondence, the idea that meaning is constructed through structured sets of differences – and recognizing the importance of critical analysis, it is argued that contextual information from the past can lead to understanding of functional and ideational meanings. In this way long-term history can be reconstructed and can contribute to debate within modern social theory and within society at large.

Bibliography

Althusser, L., 1977, *For Marx*, London: New Left Books

Ammerman, A., 1979, 'A Study of Obsidian Exchange Networks in Calabria', *World Archaeology* 11, 95–110

Arnold, D., 1983, 'Design Structure and Community Organisation in Quinua, Peru', in D. Washburn (ed.), *Structure and Cognition in Art*, Cambridge University Press

Bailey, G. (ed.) 1983, *Hunter–Gatherer Economy in Prehistory: a European Perspective*, Cambridge University Press

Barrett, J. C., 1981, 'Aspects of the Iron Age in Atlantic Scotland: a Case Study in the Problems of Archaeological Interpretation', *Proceedings of the Society of Antiquaries of Scotland* 111, 205–19

Bender, B., 1978, 'Gatherer–Hunter to Farmer: a Social Perspective', *World Archaeology* 10, 204–22

Berard, C. and Durand, J.-L., 1984, 'Entrer en imagerie', in *La Cité des images*, Paris: Fernand Nathan

Binford, L. R., 1962, 'Archaeology as Anthropology', *American Antiquity* 28, 217–25

1965, 'Archaeological Systematics and the Study of Cultural Process', *American Antiquity* 31, 203–10

1967, 'Smudge Pits and Hide Smoking: the use of Analogy in Archaeological Reasoning', *American Antiquity* 32, 1–12

1971, 'Mortuary Practices: their Study and their Potential', in J. Brown (ed.), *Approaches to the Social Dimensions of Mortuary Practices*, Memoirs of the American Archaeology Society 25

(ed.) 1977, *For Theory Building in Archaeology*, New York: Academic Press

1978, *Nunamiut Ethnoarchaeology*, New York: Academic Press

1982, 'Meaning, Inference and the Material Record', in A. C. Renfrew and S. Shennan (eds.), *Ranking, Resource and Exchange*, Cambridge University Press

1983, *In Pursuit of the Past*, London: Thames and Hudson

1984, 'An Ayawara Day: Flour, Spinifex Gum, and Shifting Perspectives', *Journal of Anthropological Research* 40, 157–82

and Sabloff, J. A., 1982, 'Paradigms, Systematics and Archaeology', *Journal of Anthropological Research* 38, 137–53

Bintliff, J. L., 1984, 'Structuralism and Myth in Minoan Studies', *Antiquity* 58, 35–8

Boas, F., 1940, *Race, Language and Culture*, New York: MacMillan Press

Bourdieu, P., 1977, *Outline of a Theory of Practice*, Cambridge University Press

Bradley, R., 1984, *The Social Foundations of Prehistoric Britain*, London: Longman

Braithwaite, M., 1982, 'Decoration as Ritual Symbol: a Theoretical Proposal and an Ethnographic Study in Southern Sudan', in I. Hodder (ed.), *Symbolic and Structural Archaeology*, Cambridge University Press

Butzer, K., 1982, *Archaeology as Human Ecology*, Cambridge University Press

Carr, C., 1984, 'The Nature of Organisation of Intrasite Archaeological Records and Spatial Analysis Approaches to their Investigation', in M. Schiffer (ed.), *Advances in Archaeological Method and Theory*, vol. 7, New York: Academic Press

Case, H., 1973, 'Illusion and meaning', in A. C. Renfrew (ed.), *The Explanation of Culture Change*, London: Duckworth

Chapman, R. W., 1981, 'The Emergence of Formal Disposal Areas and the "Problem" of the Megalithic Tombs in Prehistoric Europe', in R. Chapman, I. Kinnes and K. Randsborg (eds.), *The Archaeology of Death*, Cambridge University Press

Childe, V. G., 1925, *The Dawn of European Civilisation*, London: Kegan Paul

   1936, *Man Makes Himself*, London: Collins

   1949, *Social Worlds of Knowledge*, Oxford University Press

   1951, *Social Evolution*, New York: Schuman

Clark, J. G. D., 1939, *Archaeology and Society*, London: Methuen

Clarke, D. L., 1968, *Analytical Archaeology*, London: Methuen

   1972, 'A Provisional Model of an Iron Age Society and its Settlement System', in D. L. Clarke (ed.), *Models in Archaeology*, London: Methuen

   1973, 'Archaeology: the Loss of Innocence', *Antiquity* 47, 6–18

Coe, M. D., 1978, 'Supernatural Patrons of Maya Scribes and Artists', in N. Hammond (ed.), *Social Process in Maya History*, New York: Academic Press

Collingwood, R. G., 1939, *An Autobiography*, Oxford University Press

   1946, *The Idea of History*, Oxford University Press

   and Myres, J., 1936, *Roman Britain and the English Settlements*, Oxford University Press

Bibliography

Conkey, M. W., and Spector, J., 1984, 'Archaeology and the Study of Gender', in M. Schiffer (ed.), *Advances in Archaeological Method and Theory*, vol. 7, New York: Academic Press

Cresswell, R., 1972, 'Les Trois Sources d'une technologie nouvelle', in J. M. C. Thomas and L. Bernot (eds.), *Langues et techniques, nature et société*, Paris: Klinksieck

Daniel, G. E., 1962, *The Idea of Prehistory*, Harmondsworth: Penguin

Davis, D. D., 1984, 'Investigating the Diffusion of Stylistic Innovations', in M. Schiffer (ed.), *Advances in Archaeological Method and Theory*, vol. 6, New York: Academic Press

Davis, W., 1982, 'Canonical Representation in Egyptian Art', *Res* 4, 21–46
    1984, 'Representation and Knowledge in the Prehistoric Rock Art of Africa', *African Archaeological Review* 2, 7–35

Deetz, J., 1977, *In Small Things Forgotten*, New York: Anchor Books
    1983, 'Scientific Humanism and Humanistic Science: a Plea for Paradigmatic Pluralism in Historical Archaeology', *Geoscience and Man* 23, 27–34

Digard, J.-P., 1979, 'La technologie en anthropologie: fin de parcours ou nouveau siffle?', *L'Homme* 19, 73–104

Donley, L., 1982, 'House Power: Swahili Space and Symbolic Markers', in I. Hodder (ed.)., *Symbolic and Structural Archaeology*, Cambridge University Press

Doran, J., and Hodson, F. R., 1975, *Mathematics and Computers in Archaeology*, Edinburgh University Press

Drennan, R., 1976, 'Religion and Social Evolution in Formative Mesoamerica', in K. Flannery (ed.), *The Early Mesoamerican Village*, New York: Academic Press

Drummond, L., 1983, 'Jonestown: a Study in Ethnographic Discourse', *Semiotica* 46, 167–209

Earle, T., and Ericson, J., (eds.), 1977, *Exchange Systems in Prehistory*, New York: Academic Press

Ericson, J., and Earle, T., (eds.), 1982, *Contexts for Prehistoric Exchange*, New York: Academic Press

Faris, J., 1972, *Nuba Personal Art*, London: Duckworth
    1983, 'From Form to Content in the Structural Study of Aesthetic Systems', in D. Washburn (ed.), *Structure and Cognition in Art*, Cambridge University Press

Flannery, K. V., 1967, 'Culture History v. Culture Process: a Debate in American Archaeology', *Scientific American* 217, 119–22
    1973, 'Archaeology with a Capital S', in C. Redman

(ed.), *Research and Theory in Current Archaeology*, New York: Wiley

1982, 'The Golden Marshalltown: a Parable for the Archaeology of the 1980s', *American Anthropologist* 84, 265–78

and Marcus, J., 1976, 'Formative Oaxaca and the Zapotec Cosmos', *American Scientist* 64, 374–83

1983, *The Cloud People*, New York: Academic Press

Fletcher, R., 1977, 'Settlement Studies (Micro and Semi-Micro)', in D. L. Clarke (ed.), *Spatial Archaeology*, New York: Academic Press

Foucault, M., 1977, *Discipline and Punish*, New York: Vintage Books

Frankenstein, S., and Rowlands, M., 1978, 'The Internal Structure and Regional Context of Early Iron Age Society in South-Western Germany', *Bulletin of the Institute of Archaeology* 15, 73–112

Friedman, J., 1974, 'Marxism, Structuralism and Vulgar Materialism', *Man* 9, 444–69

1975, 'Tribes, States and Transformations', in M. Bloch (ed.), *Marxist Analyses in Social Anthropology*, London: Association of Social Anthropologists

and Rowlands, M., (eds.) 1978, *The Evolution of Social Systems*, London: Duckworth

Fritz, J., 1978, 'Paleopsychology Today: Ideational Systems and Human Adaptation in Prehistory', in C. Redman *et al.* (eds.), *Social Archaeology: Beyond Dating and Subsistence*, New York: Academic Press

Gellner, E., 1982, 'What is Structuralisme?', in C. Renfrew, M. Rowlands and B. Seegraves (eds.), *Theory and Explanation in Archaeology*, London: Academic Press

Gibbs, L., 1986, 'Identifying Gender Representation in the Archaeological Record: A Contextual Study', in I. Hodder (ed.), *The Archaeology of Contextual Meanings*, Cambridge University Press

Giddens, A., 1976, 'Introduction', in M. Weber, *The Protestant Ethic and the Spirit of Capitalism*, London: George Allen and Unwin

1979, *Central Problems in Social Theory*, London: MacMillan

1981, *A Contemporary Critique of Historical Materialism*, London: MacMillan

Gilman, A., 1984, 'Explaining the Upper Palaeolithic Revolution', in M. Spriggs, (ed.), *Marxist Perspectives in Archaeology*, Cambridge University Press

Glassie, H., 1975, *Folk Housing of Middle Virginia*, Knoxville: University of Tennessee Press

Gould, R., 1980, *Living Archaeology*, Cambridge University Press

Bibliography

Gregory, T., 1983, 'The Impact of Metal Detecting on Archaeology and the Public', *Archaeological Review from Cambridge* 2, 5–8

Hall, R. L., 1976, 'Ghosts, Water Barriers, Corn, and Sacred Enclosures in the Eastern Woodlands', *American Antiquity* 41, 360–4

1977, 'An Anthropocentric Perspective for Eastern United States Prehistory', *American Antiquity* 42, 499–517

1983, 'A Pan-continental Perspective on Red Ochre and Glacial Kame Ceremonialism', in R. C. Dunnell and D. K. Grayson (eds.), *Lulu Linear Punctuated: Essays in Honour of George Irving Quimby*, University of Michigan Anthropological Papers, 72

Handsman, R., 1980, 'Studying Myth and History in Modern America: Perspectives for the Past from the Continent', *Reviews in Anthropology* 7, 255–68

1981, 'Early Capitalism and the Centre Village of Canaan, Connecticut, a Study of Transformations and Separations', *Artifacts* 9, 1–21

Hardin, M., 1970, 'Design Structure and Social Interaction: Archaeological Implications of an Ethnographic Analysis', *American Antiquity* 35, 332–43

Harris, M., 1979, *Cultural Materialism: The Struggle for a Science of Culture*, New York: Random House

Haudricourt, A. G., 1962, 'Domestication des animaux, culture des plantes et traitement d'autrui', *L'Homme* 2, 40–50

Hawkes, C., 1942, 'Race, Prehistory and European Civilisation', *Man* 73, 125–30

1954, 'Archaeological Theory and Method: some Suggestions from the Old World', *American Anthropologist* 56, 155–68

1972,'Europe and England: Fact and Fog', *Helinium* 12, 105–16

1976, 'Celts and Cultures: Wealth, Power, Art', in C. Hawkes and P.-M. Duval, *Celtic Art in Ancient Europe*, London: Seminar Press

Hawkes, J., 1968, 'The Proper Study of Mankind', *Antiquity* 42, 255–62

Held, D., 1980, *Introduction to Critical Theory*, London: Hutchinson

Higgs, E. S., and Jarman, M., 1969, 'The Origins of Agriculture: a Reconsideration', *Antiquity* 43, 31–41

Hillier, B., Leaman, A., Stansall, P., and Bedford, M., 1976, 'Space Syntax', *Environment and Planning* Series B 3, 147–85

Hodder, I., 1979, 'Social and Economic Stress and Material Culture Patterning', *American Antiquity* 44, 446–54

1981, 'Towards a Mature Archaeology', in I. Hodder, G. Isaac and N. Hammond (eds.), *Pattern of the Past*, Cambridge University Press

1982a, *Symbols in Action*, Cambridge University Press

1982b, 'Sequences of Structural Change in the Dutch Neolithic', in I. Hodder (ed.), *Symbolic and Structural Archaeology*, Cambridge University Press

1982c, 'Theoretical Archaeology: a Reactionary View', in I. Hodder (ed.), *Symbolic and Structural Archaeology*, Cambridge University Press

1982d, *The Present Past*, London: Batsford

1984a, 'Burials, Houses, Women and Men in the European Neolithic', in D. Miller and C. Tilley (eds.), *Ideology, Power and Prehistory*, Cambridge University Press

1984b, 'Archaeology in 1984', *Antiquity* 58, 25–32

1985, 'New Generations of Spatial Analysis in Archaeology', (to be published)

(ed.), 1986, *Archaeology as Long Term History*, Cambridge University Press

1986, 'The Decoration of Containers; an Ethnographic Study', (to be published)

and Evans, C., 1984, 'Report on the Excavations at Haddenham, Cambs.', *Cambridgeshire Archaeological Committee Annual Report* 3, 11–14

and Lane, P., 1982, 'A Contextual Examination of Neolithic Axe Distribution in Britain', in J. Ericson and T. Earle (eds.), *Contents for Prehistoric Exchange*, New York: Academic Press

and Okell, E., 1978, 'An Index for assessing the Association between Distributions of Points in Archaeology', in I. Hodder (ed.), *Simulation Studies in Archaeology*, Cambridge University Press

and Orton, C., 1976, *Spatial Analysis in Archaeology*, Cambridge University Press

Parker Pearson, M., Peck, N., and Stone, P., 1985, *Archaeology, Knowledge and Society: Surveys in Britain* (typescript)

Horkheimer, M., and Adorno, T., 1973, *Dialectic of the Enlightenment*, London: Allen Lane

Huffman, T. N., 1981, 'Snakes and Birds: Expressive Space at Great Zimbabwe', *African Studies* 40, 131–50

1984, 'Expressive Space in the Zimbabwe Culture', *Man* 19, 593–612

Isbell, W. H., 1976, 'Cosmological Order expressed in Prehistoric

Bibliography

Ceremonial Centres', *Andean Symbolism Symposium*, Paris: International Congress of Americanists

Johnson, G., 1982, 'Organisational Structure and Scalar Stress', in A. Renfrew, M. Rowlands and B. Seagrave (eds.), *Theory and Explanation in Archaeology*, New York: Academic Press

Kehoe, A. B., 1979, 'The Sacred Heart: a Case for Stimulus Diffusion', *American Ethnologist* 6, 763–71

and Kehoe, T. F., 1973, 'Cognitive Models for Archaeological Interpretation', *American Antiquity* 38, 150–4

1977, 'Stones, Solstices and Sun Dance Structures', *Plains Anthropologist* 22, 85–95

Kent, S., 1984, *Analysing Activity Areas*, Albuquerque: University of New Mexico Press

Kintigh, K., and Ammerman, A. J., 1982, 'Heuristic Approaches to Spatial Analysis in Archaeology', *American Antiquity* 47, 31–63

Kohl, P. L., 1981, 'Materialist Approaches in Prehistory', *Annual Review of Anthropology* 10, 89–118

Kramer, C., (ed.), 1979, *Ethnoarchaeology*, New York: Columbia University Press

Kristiansen, K., 1984, 'Ideology and Material Culture: an Archaeological Perspective', in M. Spriggs (ed.), *Marxist Perspectives in Archaeology*, Cambridge University Press

Kroeber, A. L., 1963, *Anthropology: Culture, Patterns and Processes*, New York: Harcourt Brace Jovanowich

Lathrap, D. W., 1977, 'Our Father the Layman, our Mother the Gourd: Spinden Revisited, or a Unitary Model for the Emergence of Agriculture in the New World', in C. Reed (ed.), *Origins of Agriculture*, The Hague: Mouton

Leach, E., 1954, *Political systems of Highland Burma: a Study of Kachin Social Structure*, London: Bell

1973, 'Concluding Address', in A. C. Renfrew (ed.), *The Explanation of Culture Change*, London: Duckworth

Lechtmann, H., 1984, 'Andean Value Systems and the Development of Prehistoric Metallurgy', *Technology and Culture* 25, 1–36

Lemonnier, P., 1976, 'La Description des chaines opératoires: contribution à l'étude des systèmes techniques', *Techniques et Culture* 1, 100–51

1983, 'L'Etude des systèmes techniques, une urgence en technologie culturelle', *Techniques et Culture* 1, 11–26

1984, 'L'Ecorce battue chez Les Anga de Nouvelle-Guinée, *Techniques et Culture* 4, 127–75

Leone, M., 1978, 'Time in American Archaeology', in C. Redman *et al.*
(eds.), *Social Archaeology: Beyond Subsistence and Dating*, New York:
Academic Press

1982, 'Some Opinions about recovering Mind', *American Antiquity*
47, 742–60

1983, 'The role of Archaeology in verifying American Identity',
Archaeological Review from Cambridge 2, 44–50

1984, 'Interpreting Ideology in Historical Archaeology: the William
Paca Garden in Annapolis, Maryland', in D. Miller and C. Tilley
(eds.), *Ideology, Power and Prehistory*, Cambridge University Press

Leroi-Gourhan, A., 1943, *L'Homme et la matière*, Paris: Albin Michel

1945, *Milieu et techniques*, Paris: Albin Michel

1965, *Préhistoire de l'art occidental*, Paris: Mazenod

1982, *The Dawn of European Art*, Cambridge University Press

Longacre, W., 1970, *Archaeology as Anthropology*, Tucson: Anthropological Papers of the University of Arizona, 17

McGhee, R., 1977, 'Ivory for the Sea Woman: the Symbolic Attributes of a Prehistoric Technology', *Canadian Journal of Archaeology* 1, 141–59

Marx, K., 1971, *A Contribution to the Critique of Political Economy*,
London: Lawrence and Wishart

Meltzer, D., 1979, Paradigms and the Nature of Change in Archaeology', *American Antiquity* 44, 644–57

1981, 'Ideology and Material Culture', in R. Gould and M. Schiffer
(eds.), *Modern Material Culture, the Archaeology of US*, New York:
Academic Press

Merriman, N., 1986, 'An Investigation into the Archaeological Evidence for "Celtic Spirit" ', in I. Hodder (ed.), *Archaeology as Long
Term History*, Cambridge University Press

Miller, D., 1982a, 'Artifacts as Products of Human Categorisation
Processes', in I. Hodder (ed.), *Symbolic and Structural Archaeology*,
Cambridge University Press

1982b, 'Structures and Strategies: an Aspect of the Relationship
between Social Hierarchy and Cultural Change', in I. Hodder
(ed.), *Symbolic and Structural Archaeology*, Cambridge University
Press

1983, 'Things ain't what they used to be', *Royal Anthropological Institute Newsletter* 59, 5–7

and Tilley, C. (eds.), 1984, *Ideology, Power and Prehistory*, Cambridge
University Press

Moore, H., 1982, 'The Interpretation of Spatial Patterning in Settlement Residues', in I. Hodder (ed.), *Symbolic and Structural Archaeology*, Cambridge University Press

Moore, J. A., and Keene, A. S., 1983, 'Archaeology and the Law of the Hammer', in J. A. Moore and A. S. Keene (eds.), *Archaeological Hammer and Theories*, New York: Academic Press

Muller, J., 1971, 'Style and Culture Contact', in C. L. Riley (ed.), *Man Across the Sea*, Houston: University of Texas Press

Naroll, R., 1962, 'Floor Area and Settlement Population', *American Antiquity* 27, 587–8

Okely, J., 1979, 'An Anthropological Contribution to the History and Archaeology of an Ethnic Group', in B. C. Burnham and J. Kingsbury (eds.), *Space, Hierarchy and Society*, Oxford: British Archaeological Reports International Series, 59

O'Neale, L. M., 1932, *Yurok-Karok Basket Weavers*, University of California Publications in American Archaeology and Ethnology 32

Paddaya, K., 1981, 'Piaget, Scientific Method, and Archaeology', *Bulletin of the Deccan College Research Institute* 40, 235–64

Pader, E., 1982, *Symbolism, Social Relations and the Interpretation of Mortuary Remains*, Oxford: British Archaeological Reports International Series, 130

Parker Pearson, M., 1982, 'Mortuary Practices, Society and Ideology: an Ethnoarchaeological Study', in I. Hodder (ed.), *Symbolic and Structural Archaeology*, Cambridge University Press

1984a, 'Economic and Ideological Change: Cyclical Growth in the Pre-state Societies of Jutland', in D. Miller and C. Tilley (eds.), *Ideology, Power and Prehistory*, Cambridge University Press

1984b, 'Social Change, Ideology and the Archaeological Record', in M. Spriggs (ed.), *Marxist Perspectives in Archaeology*, Cambridge University Press

Patrik, L. E., 1985, 'Is there an Archaeological Record?', in M. B. Schiffer (ed.), *Advances in Archaeological Method and Theory*, vol. 8, New York: Academic Press

Piggott, S., 1959, *Approach to Archaeology*, Harvard: McGraw Hill
1965, *Ancient Europe*, Edinburgh University Press

Plog, S., 1978, 'Social Interaction and Stylistic Similarity', in M. B. Schiffer (ed.), *Advances in Archaeological Method and Theory*, vol. 2, New York: Academic Press

Raab, L. M., and Goodyear, A. C., 1984, 'Middle-Range Theory in Archaeology: a Critical Review of Origins and Applications', *American Antiquity* 49, 255–68

Rahtz, P., 1981, *The New Medieval Archaeology*, York: University of York

Randsborg, K., 1982, 'Rank, Rights and Resources: an Archaeological Perspective from Denmark', in C. Renfew and S. Shennan (eds.), *Ranking, Resource and Exchange*, Cambridge University Press

Rappaport, R. A., 1971, 'Ritual, Sanctity, and Cybernetics', *American Anthropologist* 73, 59–76

Rathje, W., 1978, 'Archaeological Ethnography . . . because sometimes it is better to give than to receive', in R. Gould, (ed.), *Explorations in Ethnoarchaeology*, Albuquerque: University of New Mexico Press

Renfrew, A. C., 1969, 'Trade and Culture Process in European Prehistory', *Current Anthropology* 10, 151–69

1972, *The Emergence of Civilisation*, London: Methuen

(ed.), 1973a, *The Explanation of Culture Change*, London: Duckworth

1973b, *Social Archaeology*, Southampton: Southampton University

1976, 'Megaliths, Territories and Populations', in S. J. De Lact (ed.), *Acculturation and Continuity in Atlantic Europe*, Bruges: De Tempel

1977, 'Space, Time and Polity', in J. Friedman and M. J. Rowlands (eds.), *The Evolution of Social Systems*, London: Duckworth

1982, 'Discussion: Contrasting Paradigms', in C. Renfrew and S. Shennan (eds.), *Ranking, Resource and Exchange*, Cambridge University Press

1983a, *Towards an Archaeology of Mind*, Cambridge University Press

1983b, 'Divided we stand: Aspects of Archaeology and Information', *American Antiquity* 48, 3–16

Rowlands, M., and Seagraves, B., 1982, *Theory and Explanation in Archaeology*, New York: Academic Press

Richards, C., and Thomas, J., 1984, 'Ritual Activity and Structured Deposition in Later Neolithic Wessex', in R. Bradley and J. Gardiner (eds.), *Neolithic Studies: a Review of some Current Research*, Oxford: British Archaeological Reports British Series, 133

Sahlins, M., 1972, *Stone Age Economics*, Chicago: Aldine

1981, *Historical Metaphors and Mythical Realities*, Ann Arbor: University of Michigan Press

Saxe, A., 1970, *Social Dimensions of Mortuary Practices*, unpublished Ph.D thesis, University of Michigan

Schiffer, M. B., 1976, *Behavioural Archaeology*, New York: Academic Press

Schnapp, A., 1984, 'Eros en chasse', in *La Cité des images*, Paris: Fernand Nathan

Bibliography

Schrire, C., 1980, 'Hunter–Gatherers in Africa', *Science* 210, 890–1

Shanks, M., and Tilley, C., 1982, 'Ideology, Symbolic Power and Ritual Communication: a Reinterpretation of Neolithic Mortuary Practices', in I. Hodder (ed.), *Symbolic and Structural Archaeology*, Cambridge University Press

Shennan, S., 1983, 'Monuments: an Example of Archaeologists' Approach to the Massively Material', *Royal Anthropological Institute News* 59, 9–11

Sherratt, A., 1982, 'Mobile Resources: Settlement and Exchange in Early Agricultural Europe', in C. Renfrew and S. Shennan (eds.), *Ranking, Resource and Exchange*, Cambridge University Press

Spriggs, M. (ed.), 1984, *Marxist Perspectives in Archaeology*, Cambridge University Press

Tanner, N., 1981, *On Becoming Human*, Cambridge University Press

Taylor, W., 1948, *A Study of Archaeology*, New York: Memoirs of the American Anthropological Association 69

Tilley, C., 1984, 'Ideology and the Legitimation of Power in the Middle Neolithic of Southern Sweden', in D. Miller and C. Tilley (eds.), *Ideology, Power and Prehistory*, Cambridge University Press

Tolstoy, P., 1966, 'Method in Long Range Comparison', *Congreso Internacional de Americanistas* 36, 69–89

1972, Diffusion: as Explanation and as Event', in N. Barnard (ed.), *Early Chinese Art and its Possible Influence in the Pacific Basin*, New York: Intercultural Arts Press

Trigger, B., 1978, *Time and Tradition*, Edinburgh University Press

1980, 'Archaeology and the Image of the American Indian', *American Antiquity* 45, 662–76

1984, 'Marxism and Archaeology', in J. Maquet and N. Daniels (ed.), *On Marxian Perspectives in Anthropology*, Malibu: Undena

Van de Velde, P., 1980, *'Elsloo and Hienheim: Bandkeramik Social Structure*, Analecta Praehistorica Leidensia 12, Leiden: University of Leiden

Washburn, D. (ed.), 1983, *Structure and Cognition in Art*, Cambridge University Press

Watson, P. J., Leblanc, S. J., and Redman, C. L. 1971, *Explanation in Archaeology: an Explicitly Scientific Approach*, New York: Columbia University Press

Weber, M., 1976, *The Protestant Ethic and the Spirit of Capitalism*, London: George Allen and Unwin

Wells, P. S., 1984, 'Prehistoric Charms and Superstitions', *Archaeology* 37, 38–43

Whallon, R., 1974, 'Spatial Analysis of Occupation Floors, II, the Application of Nearest Neighbour Analysis', *American Antiquity* 39, 16–34

Willey, G., 1980, *The Social Uses of Archaeology*, Murdoch Lecture (unpublished typescript), Harvard University.

1984, 'Archaeological Retrospect 6', *Antiquity* 58, 5–14

Williamson, T., and Bellamy, L., 1983, *Ley Lines in Question*, London: Heinemann

Wobst, M., 1976, 'Locational Relationships in Palaeolithic Society', *Journal of Human Evolution* 5, 49–58

1977, 'Stylistic Behaviour and Information Exchange', University of Michigan Museum of Anthropology, Anthropological Paper 61, 317–42

Woodburn, J., 1980, 'Hunters and Gatherers today and Reconstruction of the Past', in E. Gellner (ed.), *Soviet and Western Anthropology*, London: Duckworth

Wylie, M. A., 1982, 'Epistemological Issues raised by a Structuralist Archaeology', in I. Hodder (ed.), *Symbolic and Structural Archaeology*, Cambridge University Press

1985, 'The Reaction against Analogy', in M. Schiffer (ed.), *Advances in Archaeological Method and Theory*, New York: Academic Press

Wynn, T., 1979, 'The Intelligence of Later Achenlian Hominids', *Man* 14, 371–91

Yellen, J. E., 1977, *Archaeological Approaches to the Present*, New York: Academic Press

Index

Index

Index

Index

Raab, L. M. 103
Rahtz, P. 101
Randsborg, K. 19, 20–1, 22, 24, 27
Rappaport, R. A. 22
Rathje, W. 8, 12
Redman, C. L. 119
refuse deposition 2–3, 5, 13, 50, 54, 79, 120–1
relativism 169
Renfrew, A. C. *ix*, 14, 24, 29–30, 31–2, 176
Richards, C. 34, 46
ritual 4, 87, 99, 140, 151, 154; Ilchamus 107, 110, 111–12; and Marxism 60, 62, 63, 67, 68; and structuralism 41, 46, 51, 52; and systems approach 19, 20, 22, 25, 26, 28, 32
Rowlands, M. 61, 149

Sabloff, J. A. 14–16, 29
Sahlins, M. 59, 85, 86, 90
Sami 158
Saussure, F. de 34, 36, 37, 47, 48
Saxe, A. 90
Schiffer, M. B. 2, 12, 54, 120
Schnapp, A. 34
Shanks, M. 66, 74, 75
Sherratt, A. 19, 20, 22, 26, 27
spatial analysis 34, 42–4, 50, 52, 71, 73, 79; and contextual archaeology 119, 125, 129–38, 144–5, 146, 151
Spector, J. 159–60
Spriggs, M. 57
Stone, P. 161, 162
structuralism *ix*, 31, 32–54, 104; and contextual approach 118, 121, 129, 130, 132, 136; and history 78, 80, 85, 88–90, 93, 101; and Marxism 55, 58, 61, 70–6; and post-processual trends 147, 149, 152–6 *passim*, 170, 171, 173, 174
'structuration' 70–6
style 2, 5, 12, 89, 110; and contextual approach 130, 132, 133, 149; and Marxism 59, 62, 68, 75; and systems approach 19, 20, 21, 22, 26
Sudan 37
surveys, public attitude 161–3, 167
Sweden 74, 75
symbolism 3, 12, 56, 148, 154, 160; and contextual approach 118, 119, 121, 123–30 *passim*, 135–45 *passim*; and history

79, 87, 99; and Ilchamus 106, 107, 110, 116; and Marxism 62–7, 69, 75, 76; and structuralism 34, 40, 51, 52–3, 54; and systems approach 19, 20–6, 33
Symbols in Action see Hodder (1982a)
systems theory *ix*, *x*, 6–7, 12, 13, 18–33; and contextual approach 119, 120, 122, 127, 129, 135; and history 77, 78, 80; and post-processual trends 147, 149, 152, 163, 166, 170; and structuralism 34–5, 39, 40, 49, 54

taken-for-granteds 63, 113, 116, 161, 166, 170
Tanner, N. 160
Taylor, W. 79, 92, 93, 175–6
technology 55–6, 58–9, 87, 91, 153, 165, 167–8
temporal analysis 27, 128–38, 144–5, 146, 151
Thomas, J. 34, 46
Thule 45–6
Tilley, C. 50, 64, 66, 67, 74, 75
Tolstoy, P. 55
Trigger B. 16, 57, 81, 158
typology 131–4, 135, 149

U.S.A. *see* America

Van de Velde, P. 34
Vikings 19, 164
Von Daniken, Erich 161, 163

Washburn, D. 34, 36, 37, 39–40, 41
Watson, P. J. 119
Weber, Max 81–6, 90
Wells, P. S. 122
Whallon, R. 120
Willey, G. 93, 164
Williamson, T. 161
Wobst, M. 19, 21, 22, 24, 26, 61–2, 106
Woodburn, J. 77
working-class perspectives 157, 162–4, 166–7
Wylie, M. A. 35, 49, 144, 153
Wynn, T. 34

Yellen, J. E. 103
Yugoslavia 21, 24

Zapotec 20, 22, 28, 99

ALSO FROM CAMBRIDGE

Archaeology as Long-term History
Edited by Ian Hodder

In marked contrast with the anthropological and cross-cultural approaches that have featured so prominently in the archaeological research of the last twenty-five years, this contributory volume emphasises the archaeological significance of historical method and philosophy. Drawing particularly on the work of R. G. Collingwood, the contributors show that the notion of 'history seen from within' is a viable approach that can be applied in enthnoarchaeology and in both historic and prehistoric archaeology. Examination of the relationship between structure and event within historical contexts leads to new insights into the interdependence of continuity and change, and into the nature of widely recognised processes such as acculturation, diffusion and migration.

Contributors: DAVID COLLETT; ALEXANDER VON GERNET; KEVIN GREENE; KNUT HELSKOG; IAN HODDER; PAUL LANE; HENRIETTA MOORE; JAQUELINE NOWAKOWSKI; AJAY PRATAP; PETER TIMMINS; ELISABETH VESTERGAARD; JAMES WHITLEY.

New Directions in Archaeology   ISBN 0 521 32923 X

The Archaeology of Contextual Meanings
Edited by Ian Hodder

This companion volume to *Archaeology as Long-term History* focuses on the symbolism of artefacts. It seeks at once to refine current theory and method relating to interpretation and show, with examples, how to conduct this sort of archaeological work. Some contributors work with the material culture of modern times or the historic period. However, the book also contains a number of applications in prehistory to demonstrate the feasibility of symbolic interpretation where good contextual data survive from the distant past.

In relation to wider debates within the social sciences, the volume is characterised by a concern to place abstract symbolic codes within their historical context and within the contexts of social actions.

Contributors: SHEENA CRAWFORD; LIV GIBBS; IAN HODDER; ROBERT JAMESON; NICK MERRIMAN; KEITH RAY; TONY SINCLAIR; MARIE LOUISE SØRENSON; TIMOTHY TAYLOR; LINDA THERKORN; SARAH WILLIAMS.

New Directions in Archaeology   ISBN 0 521 32924 8